Four Decades of
GREAT POPULAR MUSIC

WARNER BROS. PUBLICATIONS - THE GLOBAL LEADER IN PRINT
USA: 15800 NW 48th Avenue, Miami FL 33014

WARNER/CHAPPELL MUSIC

CANADA: 85 SCARSDALE ROAD, SUITE 101
DON MILLS, ONTARIO, M3B 2R2
SCANDINAVIA: P.O. BOX 533 VENDEVAGEN.85 B
S-182 15, DANDERYD, SWEDEN
AUSTRALIA: P.O. BOX 353
3 TALAVERA ROAD, NORTH RYDE N.S.W. 2113

NUOVA CARISCH

ITALY: VIA M.F. QUINTILIANO 40
20138 MILANO
SPAIN: MAGALLANES, 25
28015 MADRID

INTERNATIONAL MUSIC PUBLICATIONS LIMITED

ENGLAND: SOUTHEND ROAD,
WOODFORD GREEN, ESSEX IG8 8HN
FRANCE: 25 RUE DE HAUTEVILLE,75010 PARIS
GERMANY: MARSTALLISTR. 8, D-80539 MUNCHEN
DENMARK: DANMUSIK, VOGNMAGERGADE 7
DK 1120 KOBENHAVNK

Project Manager: Carol Cuellar
Book Design: Ken Rehm

CONTENTS

ALL I WANNA DO

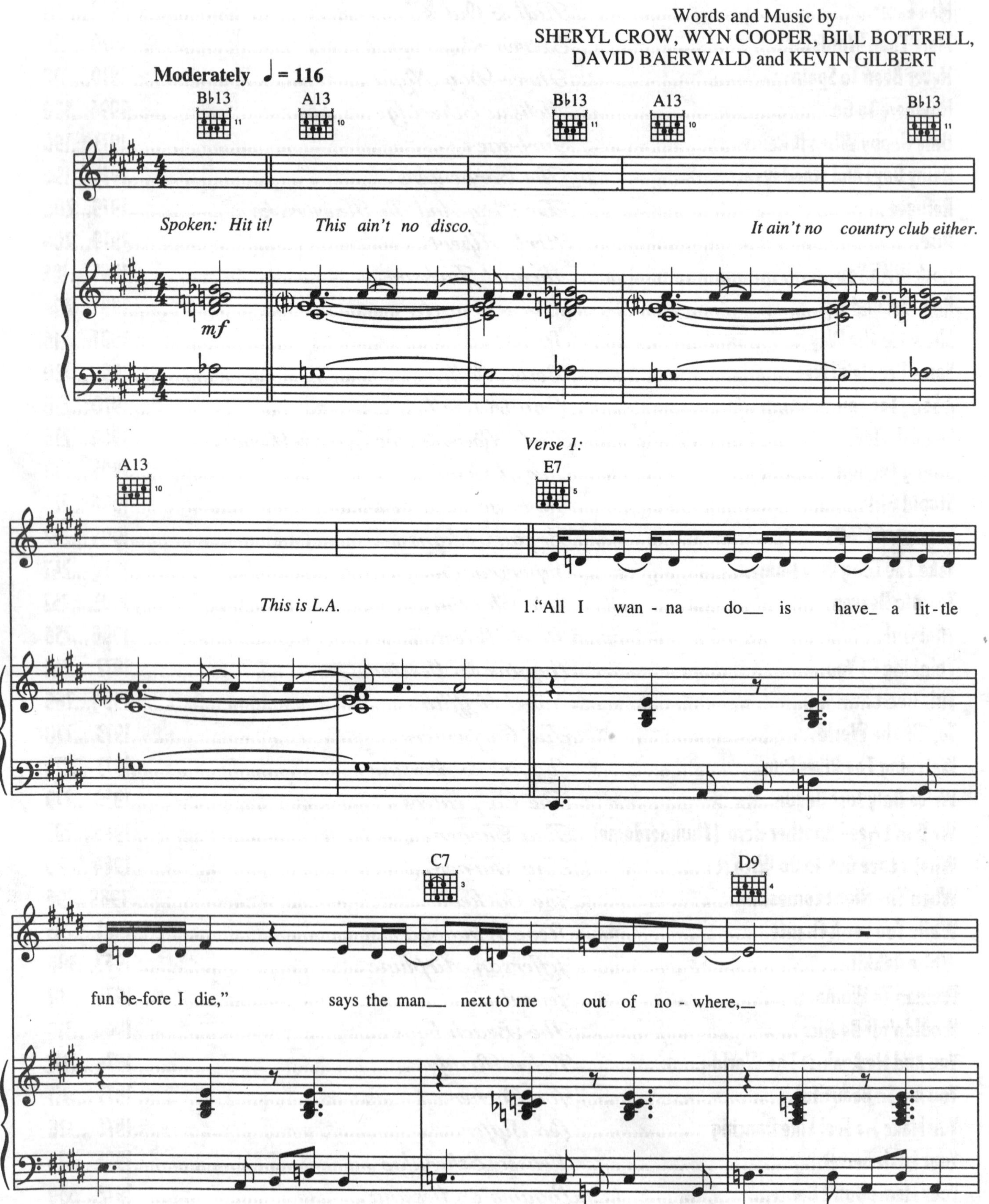

E7
a - pro - pos of noth - ing. He says his name is Wil - liam, but I'm
C7
D9
sure he's Bill or Bil - ly or Mac or Bud - dy. 2. But he's
Verses 2 & 3:
E7
plain ug - ly to me and I won - der if he's ev - er had
3. See additional lyrics.
C7
D9
E7
a day of fun in his whole life. We are drink - ing beer at

C7
D9
noon on Tues-day in a bar that fac - es a gi-ant car wash. And the
E7
good peo-ple of the world are wash - ing their cars on their lunch break,
C7
D9
hos - ing and scrub-bing as best they can in skirts and suits.
Bridge:
A13
B♭13
They drive their shin-y Dat - suns and Bu - icks

A13
B♭13
A13
back to the phone company-y, the re-cord store too._ Well, they're_ noth-ing like
Chorus:
E7
Bil-ly and me._ 'Cause all I wan-na do is have some fun,___ I got a feel-
C7
D9
E7
-ing I'm not the on - ly one. All I wan-na do is have some fun,_
C7
D9
___ I got a feel - ing I'm not the on - ly one. All I wan-na

E7
To Coda
C7
do is have some fun,
un - til the sun comes up o - ver
1. B7
E7
San - ta Mon - i - ca Boul - e - vard.
C7
D9
2. B7
San - ta Mon - i - ca Boul - e - vard.
E7
C7
D9
3

E7 C7 D9

Bridge:

A13 B♭13 A13

Oth-er-wise_ the bar___ is ours, and the day and the night and the

B♭13 A13

car wash too.____ The match-es and the Buds and the

B♭13 A13 *D.S. 𝄋 al Coda*

clean___ and dir-ty cars, the sun and the moon. But all I wan-na

Coda
C7
D9
— I've got a feel - ing the par - ty has just___ be - gun. All I wan - na
E7
C7
do is have some fun,___ I won't tell___ you that you're the on -
D9
E7
- ly one. All I wan - na do is have some fun,___ un - til the
C7
D9
E7
sun comes up o - ver San - ta Mon - i - ca Boul - e - vard,___

Verse 3:
I like a good beer buzz early in the morning,
And Billy likes to peel the labels from his bottles of Bud
And shred them on the bar.
Then he lights every match in an oversized pack,
Letting each one burn down to his thick fingers
Before blowing and cursing them out.
And he's watching the Buds as they spin on the floor.
A happy couple enters the bar dancing dangerously close to one another.
The bartender looks up from his want ads.
(To Chorus:)

ALWAYS AND FOREVER

Words and Music by
ROD TEMPERTON

Emaj9
B/C♯
C♯m7
And I know to-mor-row will still be the same,
And if you get lone-ly, call me and take
Amaj9
Emaj9
F♯m7
F♯m7/B
'cause we've got a life of love that won't ev-er change.
a sec-ond to give to me that mag-ic you make.
And
cresc.
Chorus:
Emaj9
F♯m7
G♯m7
Amaj9
G♯m7
F♯m7
ev-'ry day love me your own spe-cial way. Melt all my
mf
F♯m7/B
Emaj9
G♯m7
heart a-way with a smile.

Amaj9 G#m7 F#m7 G#m7
Take time to tell me you real - ly care and
Amaj9 G#m7 F#m7 F#m7/B Emaj9 G#m7
we'll share to - mor - row to - geth - er. Ooh ba - by,
1.
Amaj9 G#m7 F#m7 F#m7/B N.C. Emaj9 Em7/A F#m7/B
I'll al - ways love you for - ev - er. Ev - er, ev - er, ev - er!
(Al - ways for - ev - er love you.)
2.
Amaj9 G#m7 F#m7 F#m7/B N.C. Emaj9
I'll al - ways love you for - ev - er.
(Al - ways for - ev - er love

Em7/A F♯m7/B Emaj9

Ooh ba-by, ooh ba - by. Yeah ba-by, yeah ba - by. For-ev - er.
you.) (Al-ways for - ev - er love

Em7/A F♯m7/B Emaj9

Love you! Love you! You! You! Al - ways.
you.) (Al-ways for - ev - er love

Em7/A F♯m7/B Emaj9

Ev - er, ev - er, ev - er! For - ev - er.
you.) (Al-ways for - ev - er love

Em7/A F♯m7/B Emaj9

Al - ways. Oh! Ooh love, love
you.) (Al-ways for - ev - er love

Em7/A
F♯m7/B
Emaj9
you. Ev - er, ev - er, ev - er! And al - ways, I'll love
you.) (Al - ways for - ev - er love
Em7/A
F♯m7/B
Emaj9
you. Ev - er, ev - er, ev - er! Yes, I'm the one who, yes I'm the one who
you.) (Al - ways for - ev - er love
Em7/A
F♯m7/B
Emaj9
loves you al - ways.
you.) (Al - ways for - ev - er love
dim.
Em7/A
F♯m7/B
N.C.
Emaj9
For - ev - er, I'll love you.
you.)
freely
p

BACK IN THE HIGH LIFE AGAIN

Words and Music by
STEVE WINWOOD and WILL JENNINGS

Moderately, with a beat
D G(addA) D G(addA)
mf
D G(addA) D A D G(addA)
D A D G(addA) D A
It used to seem_ to me_ that my life ran on_ too fast, and I
used to be_ the best_ to make life be life_ to me, and I
D G(addA) D A
had to take_ it slow - ly just to make the good_ parts last. But
hope that you're_still out_ there and you're like you used_ to be. We'll

D
G(addA)
D
A
when you're born to run it's so hard to just slow down, so
have our-selves a time, and we'll dance till the morn-ing sun, and we'll
D
G(addA)
D
A
don't be sur-prised to see me back in that bright part of town. I'll be
let the good times come in and we won't stop un-til we're done. We'll
D
A/E
D/F♯
G
back in the high - life a-gain. All the doors I closed
D/A
A
D
A7sus4
D
A/E
one time will o-pen up a-gain. I'll We'll be back in the high life a-gain.

D/F♯ G D/A A D G/D D

— All the eyes_ that watched_ {me / us} once_ will smile and take_ {me / us} in. And {I'll / we'll}

G D A D

drink and dance_ with one_ hand free,_ {let the world_ back in - to me._ / and have the world_ so eas - i - ly._} And

G D *To Coda* 1. D/A A

oh, I'll / oh, we'll} be_ a sight_ to see___ back in the high life___ a - gain._

D G(addA) D G(addA)

—

D
G(addA)
D
A
You
2.
D/A
A
D
G
high
life
a - gain.
D
A
D
G
1.2.
D
A
3.
D.S. (lyric 2) al Coda
D
A
We'll be
Coda
D/A
A
high
life
a -

CHORUS
D7sus
G
E7
So Be True To Your School
Just like you would to your girl or guy
Em
E♭7
Be True To Your School now
And let your col-ors fly
A7
Am
1 D7
D7sus
2 D7
D7sus
Be True To Your School
2. I got a
3. On
3 D7
D7sus
G
D7sus
G
So Be True To Your School
So Be True To Your School.

THE BEST YEARS OF MY LIFE

Lyrics and Music by
WILL JENNINGS
and STEPHEN ALLEN DAVIS

C7sus
C7
D7(♭9)
Gm9
One fine day,
C6
one fine night,
Fmaj9
you lov-ing me
Am7/D
D7(♭9 ♭13)
on and on and on.
Gm9
We took our love
A7
A7(♭9 ♭13)
as far as love can
Dm7
go, ooh,
Dm7/G
G13
ooh.
B♭maj9
You've giv-en me the
1.
B♭/C
C
best years of my
F(2)
life.
B♭(2)

2.
Bb/C C Bb/C C Dm7 Dm7/G G13
best years of my life.
Bbmaj9 Bb/C C Bb/C C F(2)
You've giv-en me the best years of my life.
F/Eb
cresc.
Bridge:
Db6 Db2
mf
Bring on the storm,
Bb5/C Ab/C Db6 Db(2) Bb5/C Ab/C
we'll see it through. We'll take it all, all life can do.
Gm Am Bb/C C/D
Right to the end, we'll say, "Let's be - gin."
cresc.

Chorus:
G G/B C
You've giv - en me the best years of my life. I want to
C/D D G E7
thank you. I want to thank you.
Chorus:
A(2) A(2)/C♯ D(2)
You've giv - en me the best years of my life. I want to
D/E E C♯m7 F♯m7
thank you, thank you, thank you.
dim. mf
D E N.C. D A(2)/C♯ Bm7 A(2)
Thank you for the best years of my life.
rit. rit. e dim. mp

Verse 2:
When I play my memories again.
I feel all the pleasure and the pain.
Love can hurt, love can heal.
Oh, how we hurt and healed ourselves again.
We took our souls as far as souls can go, ooh yeah.
You've given me the best years of my life.
You've given me the best years of my life.

BREAKFAST IN AMERICA

Words and Music by
ROGER HODGSON and
RICK DAVIES

G
Fm
B♭
Fm
B♭
see the girls in Cal-i-for-nia. I'm hop-ing it's going to come true, but there's not a lot I can do.
I'm a los-er, what a jok-er. I'm play-ing my jokes up-on you while there's noth-ing bet-ter to do.
to Coda
G
Cm
Ba-ba-da-dow, ba-ba-dow-ba-ba dow-di-dow di-dow.
G
Cm
A♭
4 fr.
Ba-ba-da-dow, ba-ba-dow-ba-ba dow-di-dow di-dow. Na na na, na na
Fm
B♭
D.S. al Coda
(3rd verse)
na na na na na.
Coda
G
Ba-ba-da-dow, ba-ba-dow-ba-ba-

3rd Verse

Don't you look at my girlfriend;
 she's the only one I got.
Not much of a girlfriend,
I never seem to get a lot.

Take a jumbo 'cross the water,
 like to see America,
 see the girls in California.
I'm hoping it's going to come true,
 but there's not a lot I can do.

CALIFORNIA GIRLS

Words and Music by
BRIAN WILSON

C
The mid - west far - mers' daughters - ters real - ly
I been all 'round this. great big world and I've
C7
F
make you feel al - right. And the north - ern girls with the
seen all kinds of girls. But I could - n't wait to get
G7
way they kiss, they keep their boy - friends warm at night. I
back in the states, back to the cut - est girls in the world.
cresc.
Chorus:
C
Dm7
B♭
wish they all could be Cal - i - for - nia, I wish they all could be
f

Cm7
Ab
Bbm7
Cal - i - for - nia, I
wish they all could be
Cal - i - for - nia
1.
C
girls.
2. The
mp
2.
C
girls.
N. C.
mp
I
C
wish they all could be
mf
Cal - i - for - nia; I
F
wish they all could be
1.
Cal - i - for - nia; I
2.
F/G
C
Cal - i - for - nia
girls.

COME SAIL AWAY

Words and Music by
DENNIS DeYOUNG

F
G
Am
free to face the life that's a - head of me.
On board I'm the cap-tain,
G
Am
so climb a-board.
We'll search for to-mor-row,
G
C
Em/B
Am
Am/G
3
on ev - 'ry shore. And I'll try, oh Lord, I'll try
F
G
C
Dm
Em
Dm
to car - ry on.

C
G7
C
Em/B
Am
Am/G
I look to the sea.
F
G
Re-flec-tions in the waves spark my mem - o-ry,
C
Em/B
Am
Am/G
F
some hap-py, some sad. I think of child-hood friends and the
G
Am
G
dreams we had. We lived hap-p'ly for-ev-er so the sto - ry goes.

Am
G
But some-how we missed out on the pot of gold. But we'll
C
Em/B
Am
Am/G
F
G
try best that we can, to car - ry
C
F/C
C(add D)
F/C
C
F/C
ff
on. A gath - er-ing of an - gels ap -
ff
C(add D)
F/C
C
F/C
peared a - bove my head. They sang to me this song of hope and

C(add D)
F/C
C
F/C
this is what — they — said. — They — said
Come Sail A-way, Come — Sail A-way, Come
C(add D)
F/C
C
F/C
Sail A-way — with me — lads. —
Come Sail A-way, Come — Sail A-way, Come
C
F/C
C
F/C
Sail A-way — with me. —
Come Sail A-way, Come — Sail A-way, Come
C(add D)
F/C
C
F/C
To Coda
Sail A-way — with me. —
Come Sail A-way, Come — Sail A-way, Come

Ab
C
F/C
Sail A-way with me.
C(add D)
I thought that they were an - gels but much to my sur - prise, we
climbed a-board their star - ship and head-ed for the skies. Sing-in'
D.S. al Coda
Coda
Come Sail A-way, Come Sail A-way, Come Sail A-way with me.
Repeat and fade

COME TO MY WINDOW

Lyrics and Music by
MELISSA ETHERIDGE

D C(9) G

the hand of death. You don't know how far I'd go to

D C(9) G

use this precious ache. And you don't know how much I'd give or

D Em C(9)

how much I can take. Just to reach you. Just to reach

D Em C(9) D

you. Oh, to reach you, oh.

Chorus:

G C(9) Am D G C(9)

Come to my window. Crawl inside, wait

Am
D
G
C(9)
Am
Dsus
by the light of the moon. Come to my win - dow, I'll be home
1.
G
C(9)
Am7
D
Dsus
D
D.S. 𝄋
2.
G
C(9)
soon.
soon.
Am7
D
Dsus
D
To Next Strain
3.4. etc.
G
C(9)
Am7
Repeat ad lib. and fade
D
soon. I'll be home, I'll be home. I'm com-in' home.
Bridge:
Em
D/E
C
I don't care what they think.
I don't care what
C/B
Am
Am7
they say.
What do they know a-bout this love,

Verse 2:
Keeping my eyes open, I cannot afford to sleep.
Giving away promises I know that I can't keep.
Nothing fills the blackness that has seeped into my chest.
I need you in my blood, I am forsaking all the rest.
Just to reach you,
Just to reach you.
Oh, to reach you.
(To Chorus:)

DON'T CRY OUT LOUD

Words and Music by
PETER ALLEN and
CAROLE BAYER SAGER

F♯m7
Em7
Em7 (A bass)
clown,
and she danced with-out a net up - on the
was noth-in' more than saw - dust and some
D
F♯m (C♯bass)
Bm
wire.
glit - ter.
I know a lot a - bout her 'cause you see,
But ba - by can't be bro - ken 'cause you see,
F♯m
Bm7
E7
ba - by is an aw - ful lot like
she has the fin - est teach - er,

Em7(A bass)
A7
D
A(C#bass)
me. We don't cry out
me. An' I taught her don't cry out
Bm
Em
Em(maj7)
Em7(A bass)
A7
loud, we keep it in - side, learn how to hide our feel - ings.
loud, just keep it in - side, learn how to hide your feel - ings.
D
A(C#bass)
Bm
To Coda
Em
Em(maj7)
Fly high and proud, and if you should fall, re - mem - ber you
Em7(A bass)
Bmaj7
Em7(A bass)
D.S. al Coda
al - most had it all.

Coda
Em
Em(maj7)
Em7 (A bass)
B♭7
fall, tell me you al - most had it.
E♭
B♭(D bass)
Cm
Fm
Fm(maj7)
ff
Don't cry out loud, just keep it in - side, learn how to
Fm7(B♭bass)
B♭7
E♭
B♭(D bass)
Cm
hide your feel - ings. Fly high and proud, and if you should
Fm
Fm(maj7)
Fm7(B♭bass)
B♭7
E♭
B♭(D bass)
fall, re - mem - ber you al - most had it all. Don't

Cm
Fm
Fm(maj7)
Fm7(B♭bass)
cry_ out loud, just keep it in - side, learn_ how to hide your feel - ings.
E♭
B♭(D bass)
Cm
Fm
Fm(maj7)
Fly_ high_ and proud, and if you should fall, well ba-by you
Fm7(B♭bass)
G7
Cm
Cm(B♭bass)
A♭
A♭(B♭bass)
E♭
al - most, you al - most had it all.
D
A(C♯bass)
Bm7
Em
Em(maj7)
Em7(A bass)
Repeat and fade
mf

DON'T RUSH ME

Words and Music by
JEFF FRANZEL and
ALEXANDRA FORBES

Moderately bright rock ♩= 126

Cm
Dm
E♭
On - ly time will tell just how well I'll get to know
F
Cm
Dm
you.
Don't mean to lead you on, but I want
E♭
D7sus
D7
to take it slow- ly, slow - ly.
cresc.
Chorus:
Gm
So don't rush me.
f
Cm
D7sus
D7
I've made that mis-take be - fore, ah.
Gm
Cm
Don't rush me.
This love could be so much more; it's

Verse 2:
Desire can mean danger.
I wanna lover, not another stranger.
I'm savin' all my passion.
Who's to say if it's love, or just attraction?
Only time will tell just how well I get to know you.
Don't mean to lead you on, but I want to take it slowly, slowly.
(To Chorus:)

DON'T WORRY BABY

Words by
BRIAN WILSON, ROGER CHRISTIAN,
JAY SIEGEL, PHILIP MARGO,
HENRY MEDRESS and MITCHELL MARGO

Music by
BRIAN WILSON and ROGER CHRISTIAN

Medium Rock beat
Tacet
mf
F
Well, it's been build - in' up in - side of me for
I guess I should - a kept my mouth shut when I
She said, "Now ba - by, when you race to - day, just
Bb
C7
F
3
oh, I don't know how long.
start to brag a - bout my car.
take a - long my love with you.
I don't know
But I can't
And if you

Bb
C7
why, but I keep think - in' some-thing's bound to go wrong.
back down now be - cause I pushed the oth - er guys too far.
knew how much I loved you, ba - by, noth - ing could go wrong with you".
Gm7
C7
Am
Am7
But she looks in my eyes and makes me
She makes me come a - live and makes me
Oh what she does to me when she makes
D7
G
To Coda
Tacet
re - al - ize when she says,
wan - na drive when she says,
love to me and she says,
"Don't wor - ry,

Am
D7
G
3
ba - by,
ev - 'ry-thing will work out all right.
Tacet
1.
C7
2.
C7
D. S. al Coda
Don't wor - ry, ba - by,
oo"
oo".
Coda
Repeat and fade
Tacet
"Don't wor - ry, ba - by,
ev-'ry-thing will work out all right.
Don't wor - ry,
Repeat and fade

409

Words and Music by
BRIAN WILSON and GARY USHER

409 - 3 - 1

G
D
Gid - dy up, gid - dy up 4 0 9
When I would buy a brand
My four speed, dual quads,
C
G
4 0 9,
4 0 9.
new 4 0 9.
pos - i - trac - tion 4 0 9.
G
4 0 9,
4 0 9,
gid - dy up, gid - dy up
Gid - dy up, gid - dy up, gid - dy up 4 0 9,
C
4 0 9.
4 0 9,
4 0 9,
gid - dy up 4 0 9, gid - dy up 4 0

G D

gid - dy up, gid - dy up 4 0 9.___

9, gid - dy up 4 0... noth - ing can catch her

C G

To Coda 𝄌 *D. S.* 𝄋 *al Coda* 𝄌

noth - ing can touch my 4 0 9.___ 4 0 9.___

Coda 𝄌 G

4 0 9,___

4 0 9,___ 4 0 9.___

Repeat and fade

G

4 0 9,___ 4 0 9.___ 4 0 9,___

Gid - dy up 4 0 9, Gid - dy up 4 0

Repeat and fade

FROM A DISTANCE

Lyrics and Music by
JULIE GOLD

G D/G G Cmaj7 D Em
flight. From a dis-tance there is har - mo-ny, and it
cresc. mf
C G/B G/D D C G/B C G/B To Coda
ech-oes through the land. It's the voice of hope, it's the voice of peace. It's the
dim. mp
C D 1. G D/G C/G G
voice of ev - ery man.
C G/B D D.S. 2. G D/G G G/B Bridge: G/C C6 D
2. From a man. God is watching us. God is
cresc. mf
D7/G G D/F♯ Em Em7 Am7 C/D D G
watch-ing us. God is watch-ing us from a dis - tance.
dim. mp

G G/B C D
Em7 G/B C G/B Am Em/G D/F♯ D
D.S. 𝄋 al Coda
G D/F♯ C/E G/D C Am Em D Em D/F♯ N.C.
cresc.
mf
3. From a
mp
Coda
C D7 D/E Em D/E Em Bm/D
heart of ev - ery man. It's the
cresc.
mf
C G/B C G/B C D7
hope of hopes, it's the love of loves. This is the song of ev - ery

Verse 2:
From a distance, we all have enough,
And no one is in need.
There are no guns, no bombs, no diseases,
No hungry mouths to feed.
From a distance, we are instruments
Marching in a common band;
Playing songs of hope, playing songs of peace,
They're the songs of every man.
(To Bridge:)

Verse 3:
From a distance, you look like my friend
Even though we are at war.
From a distance I just cannot comprehend
What all this fighting is for.
From a distance there is harmony
And it echos through the land.
It's the hope of hopes, it's the love of loves.
It's the heart of every man.

FUN, FUN, FUN

Words and Music by
BRIAN WILSON and MIKE LOVE

A7
A7+
brar - y like she told her "Old man" now.
like a Ro - man char - i - ot race now.
And with her
A lot - ta
D
G
ra - di - o blast - in', goes cruis - in' just as fast as she can now.
guys try to catch her, but she leads 'em on a wild goose chase now.
D
F♯m
G
A7
And she'll have fun, fun, fun, till her dad - dy takes the T - Bird a - way.
D
G
1. D
A7
A7+
2. D
A7
2. Well, the

D
G
D
A7
A+
A-well, you
knew all a-long that your dad was get-tin' wise to you now.
And since he took your set of keys you've been
think-in' that your fun is all through now.
But you can
A7+

D
G
come a - long with me, 'cause we got - ta lot - ta things to do now.
D
F♯m
G
A7
And you'll have fun, fun, fun, now that dad - dy took the T - Bird a - way.
D
G
1.D
A7+
2.D
E7
And you'll have
And you'll have
Repeat and fade
A
D
G7
fun, fun, fun, now that dad-dy took the T-Bird a - way.
Repeat and fade

LET'S GET TOGETHER

By
CHET POWERS

Moderately
mf

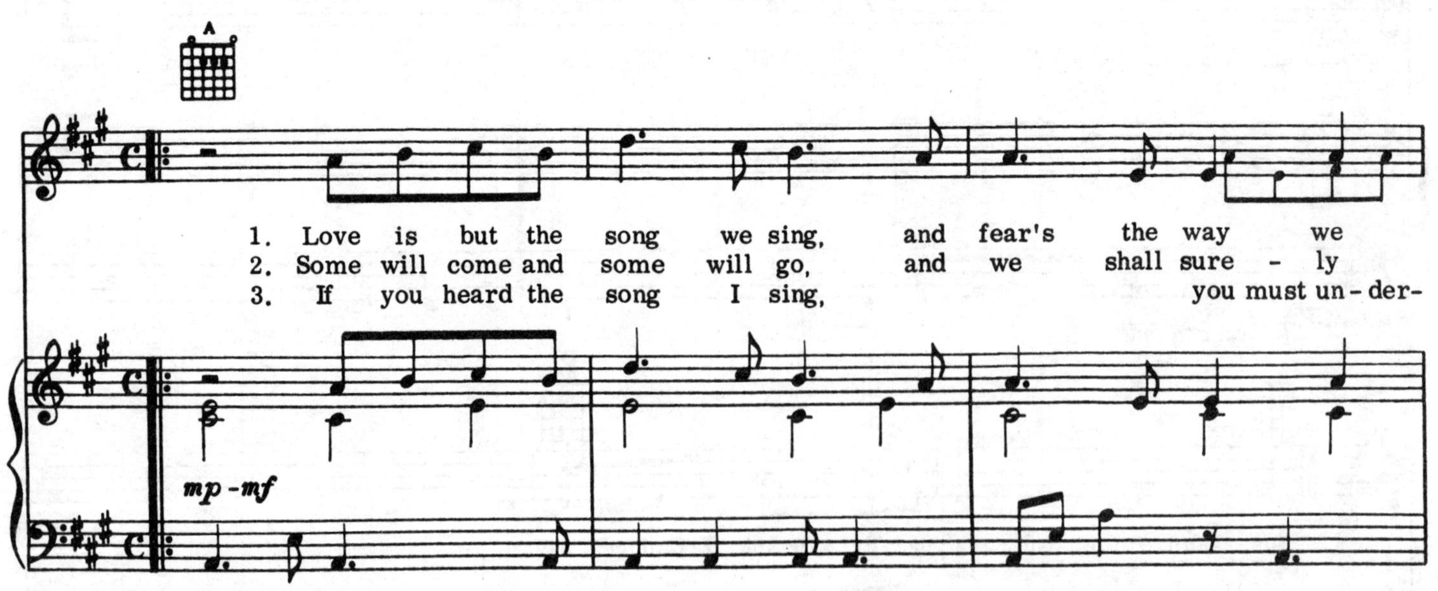
A
1. Love is but the song we sing, and fear's the way we
2. Some will come and some will go, and we shall sure - ly
3. If you heard the song I sing, you must un-der-
mp-mf

G
A
die.
pass.
stand.
You can make the
When the one who
You hold the
moun-tains ring, or make the an - gels cry.
left us here, re - turns for us at last;
key to love and fear all in your trem - bling hand,
3
3
3
Know the dove is on the wing, and
We are but a mo - ments sun - light,
One key un - locks them both you know and

G
you need not know why.
fad - ing on the grass.
it's at your com - mand.
D
E
A
C' mon peo-ple now, smile on your broth-er. Let's Get To-geth-er, try and
D
E
A
D
(A bass)
1. 2.
A
D
(A bass)
3.
A
D.S. al Coda
love one an-oth-er, right now.
Coda
A
D
(A bass)
A
D
(A bass)
A
Right now! Right now!

GOOD VIBRATIONS

Words and Music by
BRIAN WILSON and
MIKE LOVE

C
B♭
gen - tle word,
in her eyes,
On the wind that lifts her
She goes with me to a
A
C7
per - fume through the air.
blos - som world.
CHORUS
F
Cm7
I'm pick - ing up Good Vi - bra - tions, She's giv - ing me ex - ci - ta - tions.
I'm pick - ing up Good Vi - bra - tions, She's giv - ing me ex - ci - ta - tions.

G
Dm7
G
Dm7
G
Dm7
I'm pick - ing up Good Vi - bra - tions, She's giv - ing me
G
Dm7
A
Em7
A
Em7
ex - ci - ta - tions. I'm pick - ing up Good Vi - bra - tions,
1
A
Em7
A
Em7
2
A
Em7
She's giv - ing me ex - ci - ta - tions. She's giv - ing me
A
Em7
A
ex - ci - ta - tions. - ta - tions.

GIVE A LITTLE BIT

Words and Music by
RICK DAVIES and
ROGER HODGSON

Bm
Em7 (sus4)
E7
To Coda
C
There's so much _that we need ___ to share, __ so send a smile __ and show _
Now's the time _ that we need ___ to share, __ so
Bm (A bass)
A
D
A
D
A
___ you care. __
2. I'll Give A Lit - tle Bit, ______
D
G
A
G
A
G
I'll Give A Lit - tle Bit _ of my life ___ for you.

D
A
D
G
A
G
So, Give A Lit - tle Bit.
Oh, Give A Lit - tle Bit of your time to me.
A
G
Bm
Em7 (sus4)
E7
See the man with the lone - ly eyes.
Oh,
G
Bm (A bass)
A
D
A
take his hand, you'll be sur-prised.
(This Section Optional)
F♯7
Gmaj7
C
G

D.S. al Coda
Coda
A
D
G
C
Aah
Find your-self, we're on
our way back home.
Oh, go-in' home.
Don't you need, don't you need to feel at home.
Oh, yeah, we got - ta sing.

GIVE ME THE NIGHT

Words and Music by
ROD TEMPERTON

Bm7
Cmaj7
Em7
Am7
Bm7
Cmaj7
come a - live. Un - til the day is dawn - in', you can
Em7
Am7
Bm7
Cmaj7
throw out all the blues and hit the cit - y lights, 'cause there's
Chorus:
Am7
C/D
To Coda II
mu - sic in the air, and lots of lov - in' ev - 'ry-where, so give me the night.
Em7
Am7
Bm7
Cmaj7
Em7
Am7
1. Bm7
Cmaj7
Give me the night.
2. You need the

2.3.
Bm7 Cmaj7 Gm7 F Dm7 C
So come on out to-night and we'll lead the oth - ers on a
Gm7 F Dm7 C Gm7 F
ride through par - a - dise. And if you feel all right, then
Dm7 C Gm7 F E♭maj7
we can be lov - ers 'cause I see that star - light look in your eyes.
C7 E♭maj7 C/D Em7 Am7
To Coda I
Well, don't you know we can fly? So give me the night.
3
8

Verse 2:
You need the evenin' action, a place to dine,
A glass of wine, a little late romance.
It's a chain reaction.
We'll see the people of the world comin' out to dance. (To Chorus:)

Verse 3: (Instrumental solo, to Chorus:)

Verse 4:
And if we stay together,
We'll feel the rhythm of evening takin' us up high.
Never mind the weather.
We'll be dancin' in the street until the morning light.
(To Chorus:)

GOODBYE STRANGER

Words and Music by
ROGER HODGSON and
RICK DAVIES

Moderate Rock

Verse

Ab Db/Ab Ab Db/Ab Ab

It was an ear - ly morn - ing yes - ter - day, I was up be - fore the dawn. And I real - ly have en - joyed my stay, but I must be mov - in' on. Like a

I be - lieve in what you say is the un - dis - pu - ted truth. But I have to have things my own way just to keep me in my youth. Like a

Ab7/Gb
Db/F
king with - out _ a cas - tle, like a queen with - out _ a throne, _ I'm an
ship with - out _ an an - chor, like a slave with - out _ a chain, _ just the
Db
1.
Bbm
Ab
4 fr.
ear - ly morn - in' lov - er and I must be mov - in' on. _
thought of those _ sweet la - dies sends a
Now
2.
Bbm
Ab
4 fr.
Chorus
Ab7/Gb
shiv - er through _ my veins. _ And I will go on shin - ing, _ shin - in' like _ brand new. _ I'll
Db
Bbm
Ab
4 fr.
nev - er look _ be - hind _ me, _ my trou - bles will _ be few. _
(guitar 2nd time)

Abaug
Ab6
Bbm
Eb
3 fr.
Ab
4 fr.
Ab7+/Gb
Fm7
Good bye stran - ger, it's been nice.
Hope you'll find your
Tried to see your point of view,
hope your dreams will
Bbm
Eb
3 fr.
Ab
4 fr.
Ab7+/Gb
par - a - dise.
all come true.
Good - bye Mar - y, good - bye Jane.
tion, it's not for me.
Just give me mo -
1., 2.
Fm7
Bbm
Eb
3 fr.
Ab
4 fr.
Will we ev - er meet a - gain?
Feel no sor - row,
tion and set me free.
And the land and the o - cean, far a -

Ab7+/Gb
Fm7
Bbm
Eb
3 fr.
to Coda
feel no shame. Come to-mor - row, feel no pain.
way, is the life I've cho - sen, ev-'ry day. 2x And sweet de-vo -
3.
Bbm
Ab7+/Gb
Ab
4 fr.
D.S. al Coda
(3rd verse) take 2nd endings
meet a - gain?
Now
Coda
Ab
4 fr.
Ab7+/Gb
Fm7
Good - bye Mar - y, good - bye Jane. Will we ev - er
- tion it's not for me. Just give me mo - tion and set me free.
leav - in', got to go, hit the road, I'll say it once a -

Bbm
Eb
3 fr.
Ab
4 fr.
Ab7+/Gb
meet a-gain? Feel no sor - row, feel no shame.
And the land and the o - cean, far a - way, is the life I've
gain. Oh yes I'm leav - in', got to go, got to
Fm7
Bbm
Eb
3 fr.
Ab
4 fr.
Come to-mor - row, feel no pain. Good - bye Mar - y,
cho-sen ev - 'ry day. And now I'm y good-bye
go. I'm sorry I must tell you. Good-bye Mar -
Ab7+/Gb
Fm7
Bbm
Ab7/Gb
good - bye Jane. Will we ev - er meet a - gain?
Jane. Will we ev - er meet a - gain?

3rd Verse

Now some they do and some they don't
and some you just can't tell.
And some they will and some they won't.
With some it's just as well.

You can laugh at my behavior,
that'll never bother me.
Say the devil is my saviour,
but I won't pay no heed.

(TO CHORUS)

HELP ME RHONDA

Words and Music by
BRIAN WILSON
Medium rock
VERSE
F
Bb
1. Since she put me down I've been out do-in' in my head,
2. gon-na be my wife and I was gon-na be her man,
Come in late at night and in the morn-in' I just lay in bed;
But she let an-oth-er guy come be-tween us and it ruined our plans;
Well,
Well,
Dm
D7
Rhon-da you look so fine, And I know it would-n't take much time, For you to
Rhon-da you caught my eye, And I'll give you lots of rea-sons why, You got-ta

Gm7
C7
F
help me, Rhon - da, Help me get her out of my heart.
CHORUS
C7
F
Help me, Rhon - da! Help, Help me, Rhon - da! Help me, Rhon - da!
mf
C7
Help, Help me, Rhon - da! Help me, Rhon - da! Help, Help me, Rhon - da!
F
B♭
Help me, Rhon - da! Help, Help me, Rhon - da! Help me, Rhon - da!

F
Help, Help me, Rhon - da! Help me, Rhon - da! Help, Help me, Rhon - da!
Gm7
C9
1
F
Help me, Rhon-da! Yeah, get her out of my heart.
2. She was
mf
2
F
C7
Help me, Rhon - da!
f
F
Repeat and fade out
Help, Help me, Rhon - da! Help me, Rhon - da! Help, Help me, Rhon - da!

HIGHER LOVE

Words and Music by
STEVE WINWOOD and WILL JENNINGS

Dm
C
Things look so bad ev - 'ry - where.
In this whole world,
Am
B♭
C
B♭
F
what is fair?
We walk blind and we try to see,
C
Am
Dm
B♭
F
fall - ing be - hind in what could be.
Bring me a high - er love,
C
Dm7
B♭
F
C
Dm7
bring me a high - er love,
whoa.

B♭
F
C
Dm7
1.
B♭
F
Bring me a high - er love.
Where's that high - er love I keep
I could
Dm7
C
2. B♭
F
Dm7
C
think - ing of. Worlds are turn - rise a - bove on a high - er love.
B♭
C
Dm
C
B♭
C
Dm
I will wait for it. I'm not too
C
B♭
C
Dm
C
B♭
late for it. Un - til then, I'll sing my song

C
Dm
C
B♭
Dm
to cheer the night a - long. Bring it.
C
I could light the night up with my soul on fire.
B♭
Dm7
I could make the sun - shine from pure de - sire. Let me feel that

Eb
Bb
Dm
Bb
F
C
love come o - ver me.
Let me feel how strong it could be.
No chord
Oh.
Repeat and fade (vocal ad lib)
Bb
F
C
Dm7
Bb
F
C
Dm7
Bring me a high - er love,
bring me a high-er love,
whoa.
Bb
F
C
Dm7
Bb
F
C
Dm7
Bring me a high - er love,
bring me a high - er love.

HOOK

Words and Music by
JOHN POPPER

Moderately slow ♩ = 80
A
E
F♯m
C♯7
mf (Harmonica solo 2nd time)
D
A
D
E
Verse:
A
E
F♯m
C♯7
1. It does - n't mat - ter what I say, yeah,
2.3. See additional lyrics
D
A
D
E
so long as I sing with in - flec - tion

A
E
F♯m
C♯7
that makes you feel_ that I'll_ con - vey_
D
A
D
E
some in - ner truth_ of vast_ re - flec - tion._
A
E
F♯m
C♯7
But I've said noth-ing so_ far,_
D
A
D
E
and I can keep_ it up_ for as long_ as it takes._

A
E
F♯m
C♯7
And it don't mat - ter who you are.
D
A
D
E
If I'm do - in' my job, then it's your re - solve that breaks, be-cause the
Chorus:
A
E
F♯m
C♯7
hook brings you back.
(Bkgrd.)(Hook brings you back.)
D
A
D
E
A
E
I ain't tell-in' you no lie. The hook brings you back.
(Hook brings you

F♯m
C♯7
D
A
To Coda
back.)
On that you can re -
1.
D.S. al Coda
2.
Fine
D
E
D
E
A
ly.
ly.
rit.
rit.
Coda
D
E
A
E
ly.
(Harmonica solo...
F♯m
C♯7
D
A

Verse 2:
There is something amiss;
I am being insincere.
In fact, I don't mean any of this.
Still, my confession draws you near.
To confuse the issue, I refer
To familiar heroes from long ago.
No matter how much Peter loved her,
What made the Pan refuse to grow was the...
(To Chorus:)

Verse 3:
Suck it in, suck it in, suck it in if you're Rin Tin Tin or Anne Boleyn.
Make a desp'rate move or else you'll win and then begin to
See what you're doing to me, this MTV is not for free.
It's so P. C. it's killing me, so desp'rately I sing to thee of love.
Sure, but also rage and hate and pain and fear of self,
And I can't keep these feelings on the shelf.
I've tried, well, no, in fact I lied.
Could be financial suicide but I've got too much pride inside to hide or slide.
I'll do as I'll decide and let it ride until I've died and
Only then shall I abide this tide of catchy little tunes,
Of hip, three-minute ditties.
I wanna bust all your balloons, I want to burn all of your cities
To the ground. I've found I will not mess around unless I
Play, then hey, I will go on all day.
Hear what I say. I have a prayer to pray, that's really all this was.
And when I'm feeling stuck and need a buck, I don't rely on luck because the...
(To Chorus:)

I AM WOMAN

Words by
HELEN REDDY

Music by
RAY BURTON

CHORUS
F
B♭
Yes, I am wise but it's wis - dom born of pain.
mf
F
B♭
Am
Gm7
Yes, I paid the price but look how much I gained. If I have to I can do
F
Gm7
F
(A bass)
To Coda
B♭
an-y-thing. I am strong, I am in-vin-ci-ble, I am wom-an.
G
VERSE
Gmaj7
C
2. You can bend but nev - er break me 'cause it
3. I am wom-an, watch me grow see me
mp

Bm7
Em
C
on - ly serves to make me more de - ter - mined to a - chieve my fi - nal goal.
stand - ing toe to toe as I spread my lov - in' arms a - cross the land.
Dsus
D
Gmaj7
C
Gmaj7
Cmaj7
And I come back ev - en strong - er, not a nov - ice an - y long - er, 'cause you've
But I'm still an em - bry - o with a long, long way to go un -
A
1.
D
C
2.
D
C
D.S. al ⊕ Coda
deep - ened the con - vic - tion in my soul. Oh,
'til I make my broth - er un - der - stand. Oh,
⊕ Coda
B♭maj9
B♭6
B♭maj9
B♭6
B♭maj9
B♭6
wom - an! I am wom - an! I am wom - an!

HOW WILL I KNOW

Words and Music by
GEORGE MERRILL, SHANNON RUBICAM,
and NARADA MICHAEL WALDEN

1.
2.3.
D
G
2. Oh, I lose
f
How will I know?
G(9)/B
Am11
C
(Girl, trust your feel - ings.) How will I know?
How will I know? (Love can be de - ceiv - in'.) How will I know?
G/B
Chorus:
Bm7
Cmaj7
Em
How will I know if he real - ly loves me?
G/D
I say a prayer with ev - ery heart - beat.
I fall in love when - ev -

Em7
G
Bm7
Cmaj7
D
G/D
D
G/D
G
-er we meet.
I'm ask-in' you, 'cause you know a-bout these things.
G
Bm7
Cmaj7
D
Em
G
Bm7
Cmaj7
How will I know if he's think-in' of me?
I try to phone, but I'm
D
G/D
D
G/D
G
Bm7
Cmaj7
D
Em
too shy. (Can't speak.)
Fall-ing in love is so bit-ter-sweet.
G
Bm7
Cmaj7
1.
D
G/D
D
G
D.S.
2.
To next strain
D
G/D
D
G/B
C/D
This love is strong. Why do
I feel weak? 3. Oh, wake
I feel weak? If he loves
3.4. etc.
Repeat ad lib. and fade
D
G/D
D
G/D
G
G/D
G/B
C/D
I feel weak?
me;
if he loves

Verse 3:
Oh, wake me, I'm shakin'; wish I had you near me now.
Said there's no mistakin'; what I feel is really love.
How will I know? (Girl, trust your feelings.)
How will I know?
How will I know? (Love can be deceiving.)
How will I know?

**Repeat Chorus in key of "E"*

I CAN'T GO FOR THAT
(No Can Do)

Words and Music by
SARA ALLEN, DARYL HALL
and JOHN OATES

Am7
Cm7
D
F
You got the bod - y now you want my soul,
Use the bod - y now you want my soul,
Am7
Cm7
F
Ab
G
Bb
Don't e - ven think a - bout it, say no go.
Ooo for - get a-bout it now, say no go.
And
A
C
Amaj7
Cmaj7
A7
C7
I'll,
I'll do an - y - thing that you want me
Dmaj7
Fmaj7
D6
F6
A
C
Amaj7
Cmaj7
small notes
2nd & 3rd times
to. And I'll do al-most an - y

A7
C7
Dmaj7
Fmaj7
D6
F6
thing that you want me to, Yeah, but
Dm9
Fm9
I Can't Go For That, no,
Am11
Cm11
no can do. I
Dm9
Fm9
Can't Go For That, no,
Am11
Cm11
no can do. I
Dm9
Fm9
Can't Go For That, no,
Am11
Cm11
no can do. I

Dm9
Fm9
To Coda
Am11
Cm11
D.S. al Coda
_ Can't Go For That, Can't go for that, _ can't go for that, _ can't go for that.
_ can't go for that, _ can't go for that.
CODA
_ can't go for that, _ can't go for that _
(solo)
I _ Can't Go For That, _ no, _
no can do. I _ Can't Go For That, _ no, _
no can do. I _
Repeat and Fade

I CAN'T MAKE YOU LOVE ME

Lyrics and Music by
MIKE REID and ALLEN SHAMBLIN

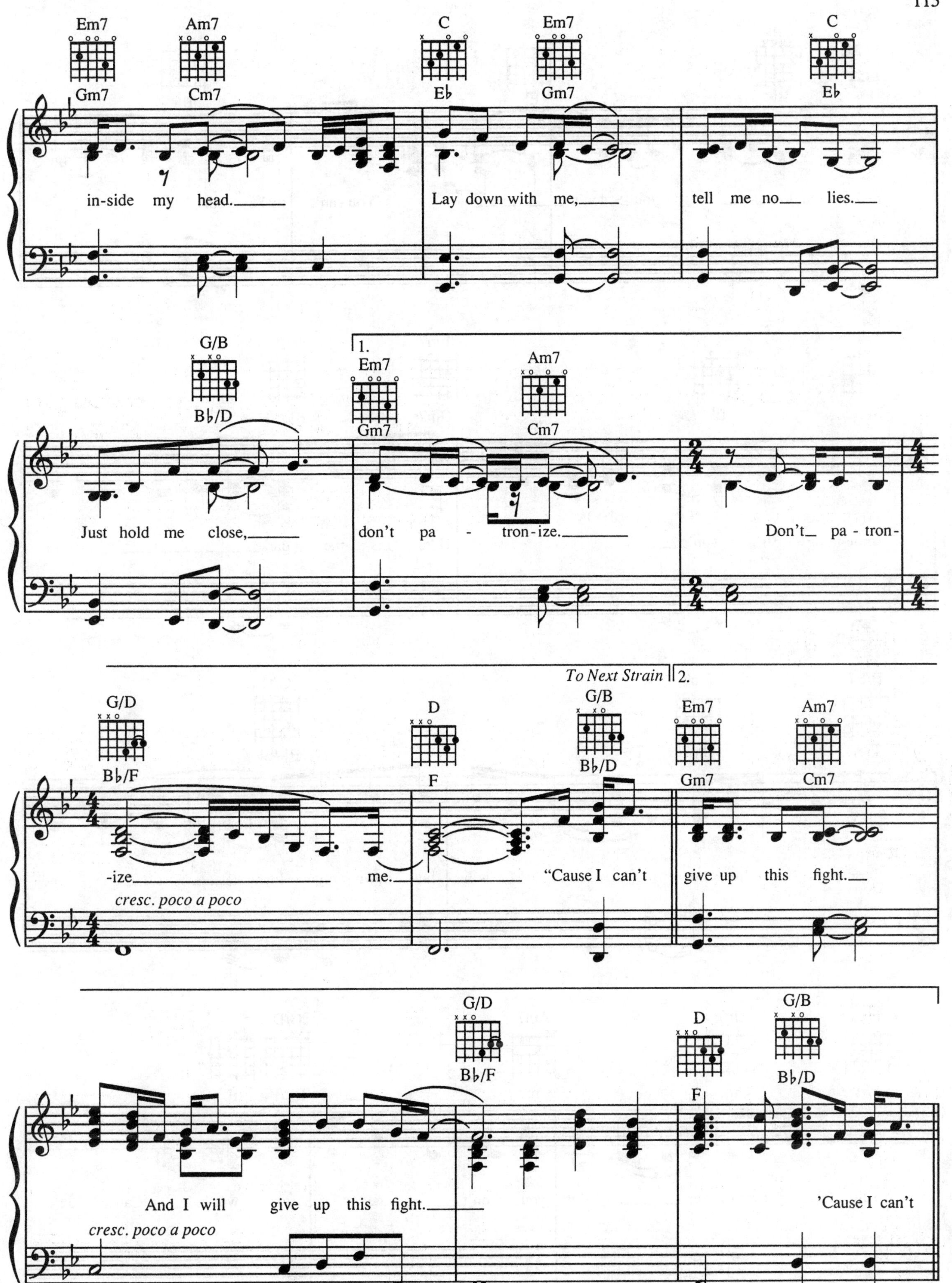
Em7
Am7
C
Em7
C
Gm7
Cm7
E♭
Gm7
E♭
in-side my head.
Lay down with me,
tell me no lies.
G/B
B♭/D
1.
Em7
Am7
Gm7
Cm7
Just hold me close,
don't pa - tron-ize.
Don't pa - tron-
To Next Strain
2.
G/D
B♭/F
D
F
G/B
B♭/D
Em7
Gm7
Am7
Cm7
-ize
me.
"Cause I can't
give up this fight.
cresc. poco a poco
G/D
B♭/F
D
F
G/B
B♭/D
And I will give up this fight.
'Cause I can't
cresc. poco a poco

Chorus:
C G C G
E♭ B♭ E♭ B♭
make you love me if you don't. You can't make your heart feel
mf
G/B C Em7 G/C
B♭/C E♭ Gm7 B♭/E♭
some-thing it won't. Here in the dark in
D/F♯ Em7 G/C
F/A Gm7 B♭/E♭
these fi - nal ho - urs, I will lay down my heart and
D/F♯ Em7 Am7 G/D D
F/A Gm7 Cm7 B♭/F F
I'll feel the pow - er. But you won't no, you won't. 'Cause I can't

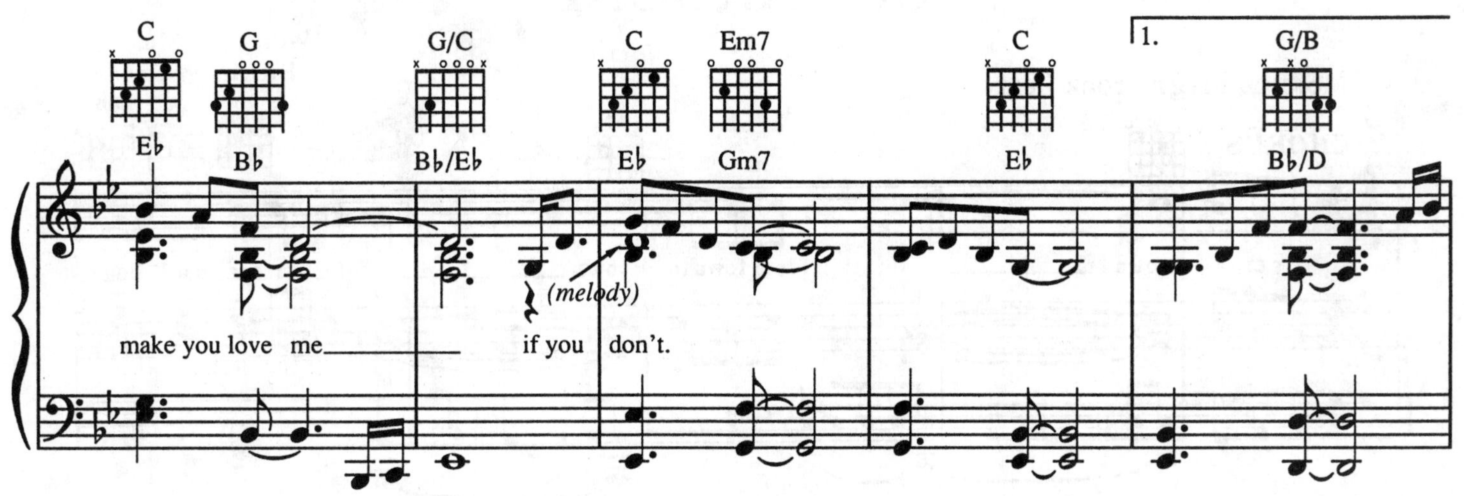

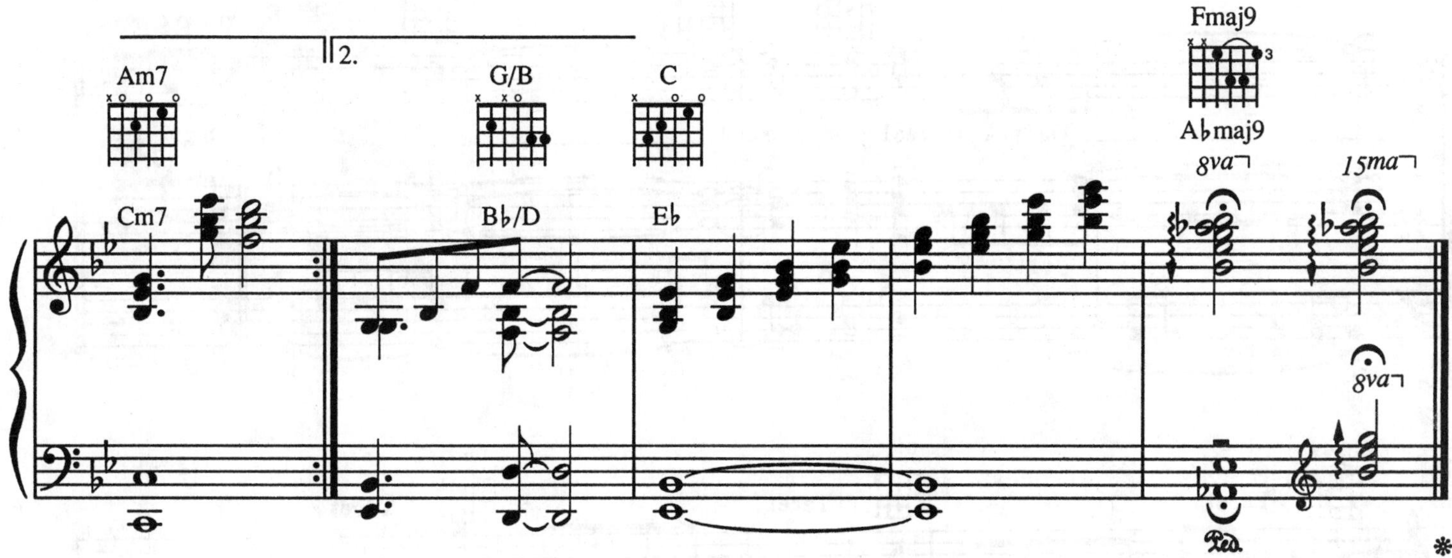

Verse 2:
I'll close my eyes, then I won't see
The love you don't feel when you're holdin' me.
Mornin' will come and I'll do what's right.
Just give me till then to give up this fight.
And I will give up this fight.
(To Chorus:)

I GET AROUND

Words and Music by
BRIAN WILSON

G7
Tacet
Dm7
Tacet
G7
Tacet
real well - known, Yeah, the bad guys know us and they leave us a - lone.
would-n't be right to leave your best girl home on a Sat - ur - day night.
CHORUS
C
A7
I get a - round from town to town
Dm
A
Dm
C
B♭
I'm a real cool head I'm mak-in' real good bread.
1
G7
2
G7
C
Repeat till fade-out
Am
2. We
Spoken I get around, etc.

I HONESTLY LOVE YOU

Words and Music by
PETER ALLEN
and JEFF BARRY

Slowly
8va
8va

B♭
F (B♭bass)
May-be I hang a-round here a lit-tle more than I should we
you don't have to an - swer I see it in your eyes
rit.

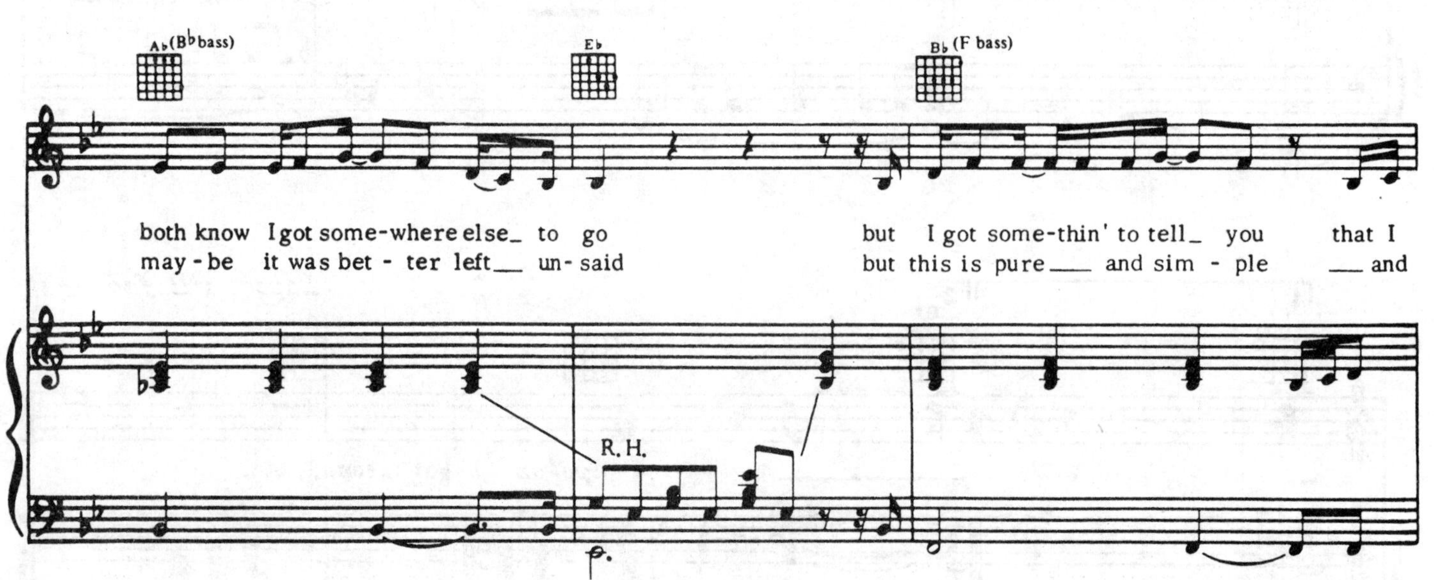
A♭(B♭bass)
E♭
B♭(F bass)
both know I got some-where else to go but I got some-thin' to tell you that I
may-be it was bet - ter left un-said but this is pure and sim - ple and
R.H.

C7
Eb
Bb(D bass)
Cm7
F7
nev-er thought I would but I be-lieve you real-ly ought to know
you must re - a-lize that it's com -in' from my heart and not my head
Bb
F (Bbbass)
Eb (Bbbass)
1. Bb
I love you
I hon-est-ly love you.
F (Bbbass)
Eb (Bbbass)
2. Bb
(Bbbass)
F (Bbbass)
Ab
Bb
you.
Eb
F (Ebbass)
Dm7
Gm7
Cm7
F7
I'm not tryin' to make you feel un - comf'-ta-ble
I'm not tryin' to make you an - y-thing at

B♭
Am7
D7
Gm7
B♭(F bass)
F (E♭bass)
E♭
all but this_ feel-ing does-n't come_ a-long_ ev-'ry day_ and you
E♭
B♭(D bass)
Cm7
Cm7 (F bass)
B♭
should-n't blow_ the chance_ when you got the chance_ to say I love you_
F (B♭bass)
E♭(B♭bass)
E♭m(B♭bass)
SPOKEN
I love you
I hon-est-ly love_
B♭
F#7
B
_ you._
If we both_were born_ in an-

F♯ (B bass)
A (B bass)
E
oth - er place and time
this mo-ment_ might be end-ing_ with a kiss
but
B (F♯bass)
C♯7
E
B (D♯bass)
there you are_ with yours_
and here I am_with mine
so I guess we'll just_ be leav-ing it_ at
C♯m7
C♯m7 (F♯bass)
B
F♯ (B bass)
F (B bass)
this
I love you_
I hon-est-ly love
B
F♯ (B bass)
E (B bass)
B
you_
I hon-est-ly
love you.
F♯ (B bass)
E (B bass)
B
8va
rit.

I WANNA DANCE WITH SOMEBODY (WHO LOVES ME)

Words and Music by
GEORGE MERRILL and
SHANNON RUBICAM

C
F/A
C/Bb
F/Bb Bb
Gm7
F/A
C/D
— till now; — it's the light of day — that shows — me how. — But when the night — falls —
Bb F/A Bb C
Chorus:
F
3
— lone - li - ness calls.
f
Oh, — I wan - na dance — with some - bod - y.
I wan - na feel the heat with some - bod - y.
Dm7
Yeah, — I wan - na dance
Bbmaj7
C7sus
— with some - bod - y, with some - bod - y who loves — me.
F
Oh, — I wan - na dance — with some - bod - y. I wan - na feel the heat

Verse 2:
I've been in love and lost my senses
Spinning through the town.
Sooner or later the fever ends,
And I wind up feeling down.
I need a man who'll take a chance
On a love that burns hot enough to last.
So when the night falls,
My lonely heart calls.
(To Chorus:)

Verse 3:
I need a man who'll take a chance
On a love that burns hot enought to last.
So when the night falls,
My lonely heart calls.
(To Chorus:)

I WON'T LAST A DAY WITHOUT YOU

Lyrics by
PAUL WILLIAMS
Music by
ROGER NICHOLS
Moderately
G
Bm7
Day af - ter day I must
So man - y times when the
C
C (D bass)
Em9
Am7
Am7(D bass)
D
face a world of stran-gers where I don't be-long, I'm not that strong.
ci - ty seems to be with - out a friend - ly face, a lone-ly place.
G
Bm7
C
C (D bass)
it's nice to know that there's some - one I can turn to who will
it's nice to know that you'll be there if I need you and you'll

Em9
Am7
Am7(D bass)
G
F(G bass)
al-ways care, you're al-ways there,
al-ways smile, it's all worth while,
When there's no get-ting ov-er that
C(add 9)
Am7
Am7(D bass)
G
F(G bass)
C(add 9)
Am7
Am7(D bass)
rain - bow, when my small - est of dreams won't come true, I can
G
F(G bass)
Cmaj7
G(B bass)
take all the mad - ness the world has to give, but I
Am7
Am7(D bass)
1.
G
G(add 9) (B bass)
C
C(D bass)
D
won't last a day with - out you.

2.
G(add 9)
Em7
A7
Dmaj7
you. Touch me and I end up sing-ing,
Em7
A7
B(sus 4)
B
C#m7
F#7
trou-bles seem to up and dis-ap-pear, you touch me with the love you're
B
G#m7
Amaj7
B(sus 4)
B
bring-ing, I can't real-ly lose when you're near. When you're
Am7
D7
G
Bm7
near my love, if all my friends have for-

C
C (D bass)
Em9
-got - ten half their prom - is - es they're not un - kind, just
Am7
Am7 (D bass)
G
Bm7
hard to find. One look at you and I
C
C (D bass)
Em9
know that I could learn to live with - out the rest, I
Am7
Am7 (D bass)
G
F (G bass)
C (add 9)
Am7
Am7 (D bass)
found the best, When there's no get - ting ov - er that rain - bow When my

G
F (G bass)
C (add 9)
Am7
Am7 (D bass)
small - est of dreams won't come true. I can
G
F (G bass)
Cmaj7
G (B bass)
take all the mad - ness the world has to give, but I
1. Amaj7
Am7 (D bass)
G (add 9) (D bass)
Am7 (D bass)
2. Am7
D7 (sus 4)
won't last a day with-out. When There's Won't last a day
G
G (add 9) (B bass)
C (add 9)
C (add 9) (D bass)
D
G (add 9)
with-out you.
poco rit.

IF I WANTED TO

Lyrics and Music by
MELISSA ETHERIDGE

*Vocal is sung one octave lower.

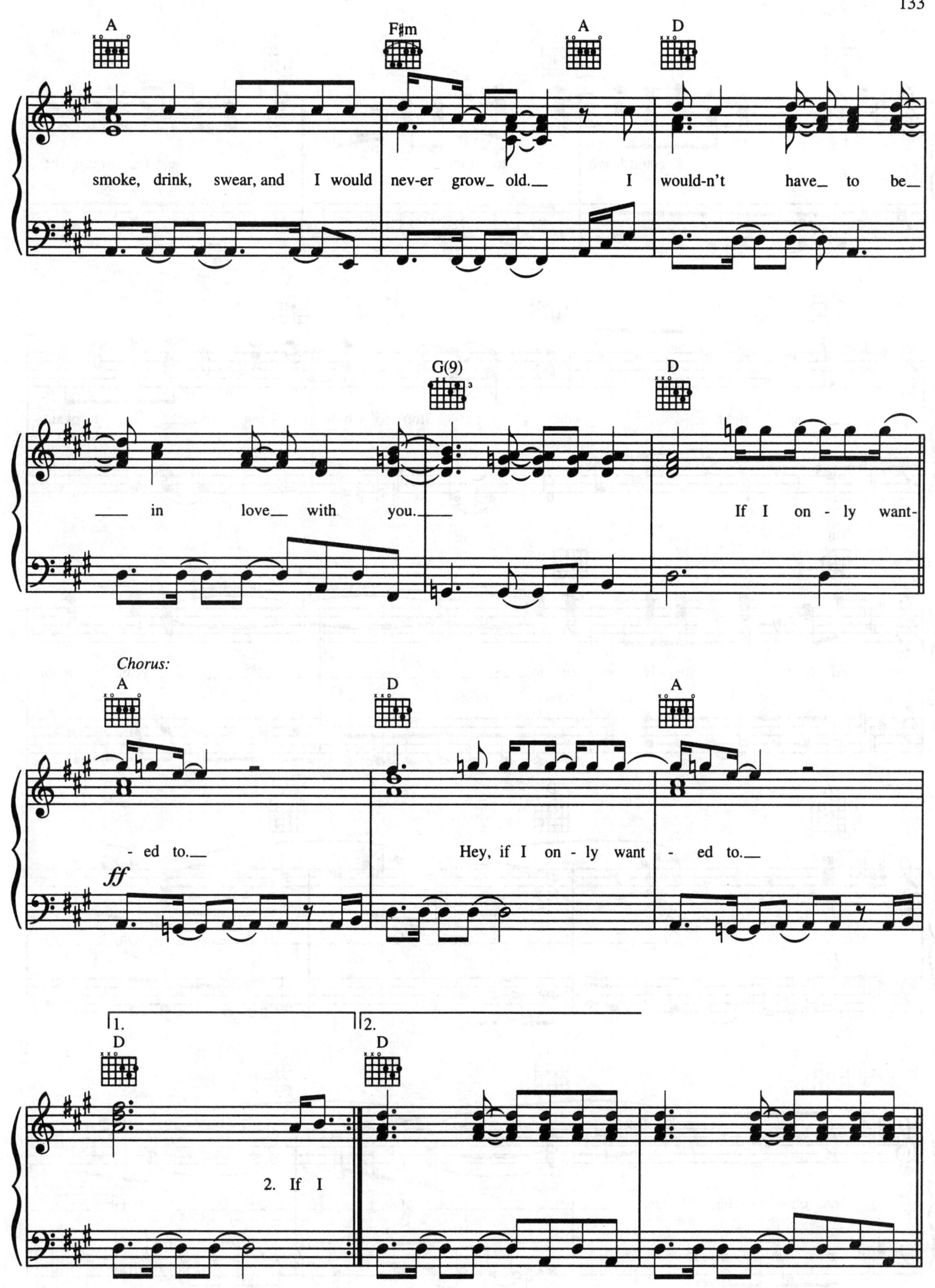
A
F♯m
A
D
smoke, drink, swear, and I would nev-er grow_ old._ I would-n't have_ to be_
G(9)
D
_ in love_ with you._ If I on-ly want-
Chorus:
A
D
A
ff
-ed to._ Hey, if I on-ly want-ed to._
1.
D
2. If I
2.
D

Bridge:
F♯m
A
Bm
f
I could leave to - night
and I would be
D
F♯m
A
all right.
Stop hold - ing on, if I want -
Bm
E
ed to, if I on - ly want - ed to,
yeah, yeah.
cresc.
A
D
A
ff
Oh.
Oh.
Oh,
D
A
D
oh, oh, oh, oh. Oh.
Oh.
Oh.

Verse 3:
G(9)
D
A
3. If I want-ed to I could be as
mf
D
A/C♯
D
pa-tient as death. Fix this hole in my heart leak-ing in-to my flesh. If I
F♯m
D
want-ed to I could turn sparks in-to ice. There'd nev-er
A
F♯m
A D
be an-oth-er wom-an who could make you think twice. I would-n't have to be
f
G(9)
D
in love with you. If I on-ly want-

Verse 2:
If I wanted to I could run fast as a train;
Be as sharp as a needle that's twisting your brain.
If I wanted to I could turn mountains to sand;
Have political leaders in the palm of my hand.
I wouldn't have to be in love with you.
(To Chorus:)

IN THIS LIFE

Words and Music by
MIKE REID and
ALLEN SHAMBLIN

Slowly ♩ = 60
C
F/A
G/B
mp
(with pedal)
Csus
C
Verse:
C
F
1. For all I'd been blessed with in my life,
G7sus
G
C
G/B
there was an emp - ti - ness in me.
Am
Dm
I was im - pris - oned by the pow - er of gold.

G7sus
C
With one hon - est touch you set me free.
Let the
cresc.
Chorus:
Dm
G/B
C
F
world stop turn - ing, let the sun stop burn - ing. Let them
mf
Dm
G7sus
G
C/E
tell me love's not worth go - ing through. If it
F
G/B
C
C/E
F
all falls a - part, I will know deep in my heart the

Verse 2:
For every mountain I have climbed.
Every raging river crossed,
You were the treasure that I longed to find.
Without your love I would be lost.
(To Chorus:)

JACKIE BLUE

Words and Music by
LARRY LEE and STEVE CASH

Moderately
Tacet
mf
Ebm7
6fr
Oo,
Oo,
Oo,
Abm7
4fr
Ebm7
6fr
Abm7
4fr
Jack - ie Blue lives her life from in - side of a room,
Jack - ie Blue, what's a game, girl, if you nev - er lose?
Jack - ie Blue likes a dream that can nev - er come true.

Ebm7
Abm7
Ebm7
hides a smile when she's wear - in' a frown; oo, Jack - ie,
Ask a win - ner and you'll prob - 'bly find, oo, Jack - ie, they've
Mak - ing love is like sift - in' through sand; oo, Jack ie, it
Abm7
G
C
G
C
you're not so down. You like your life in a free-form style;
lost at some time. Don't try to tell me that you're not a - ware
slips through your hand. Ev - 'ry day in your in - di - go eyes
Dm7
Cmaj7
G
C
you'll take an inch but you'd love a mile. There nev - er seems to be
of what you're do - ing and that you don't care. You say it's eas - y, just a
I watch the sun set but I don't see it rise. Moon-light and stars in your
G
C
Dm7
1.
Cmaj7
Tacet
quite e - nough float - ing a - round to fill your lov-in' cup.
nat - 'ral thing like play - ing mu - sic, but you
straw - ber - ry wine; you'd take the world but you

2.
Cmaj7
Tacet
Ebm7
6fr
Abm7
4fr
nev - er sing.
won't take the time.
Oo,
Oo,
Jack - ie Blue,
Jack - ie Blue
making wishes that never come true,
lives her life from inside of a room,
going places where
makes you think that her
you've never been;
life is a drag;
oo, Jack - ie, you're go - ing a - gain.
oo, Jack - ie, what
To Coda
D. S. (no repeats) al Coda
Repeat and fade
Coda
fun you have had.
Oo, Jack - ie.
Repeat and fade

JOY TO THE WORLD

Lyrics and Music by
HOYT AXTON

D
A
JOY TO THE WORLD. All the boys and
D
D7
G
Bb
girls now. Joy to the fish-es in the deep blue sea,
D
A7
To Coda
D
C
Db
D
D
Joy to you and me.
D
A
D
D7
G7
Bb
D
D. S. al Coda
C
Db
D
You

CODA
D
E
A
JOY TO THE WORLD.
All the boys and girls.
JOY TO THE WORLD,
Joy to you and me.
JOY TO THE
D7
WORLD.
All the boys and girls.
Joy to the fish-es in the
G7
Bb
Repeat and Fade
deep blue sea,
Joy to you and me.

THE LADY IN RED

Words and Music by
CHRIS DeBURGH

Gm
Bb7/F
Eb
Cm7
mance, giv-en half a chance. I have nev-er seen that dress you're wear-ing, or the
F7
Gm
high-lights in your hair that catch your eyes. I have been blind
Chorus:
F
F7/Eb
Bb
Bb/D
Ebadd2
F
The la - dy in red is danc - ing with
mf
Gm
F/A
Gm
me, cheek to cheek. There's no - bod - y here,

Cm7
Fadd9
B♭
it's just you and me.
It's where I wan-na be.
B♭7
E♭
D7/F♯
D7
But I hard - ly know
this beau- ty by my side.
cresc.
f
Gm
Gm/F
C7/E
Cm7
I'll nev- er for - get
dim.
mf
Fadd9
F
B♭
D.S.
the way you look to - night.
dim.
p

Verse 2:
I've never seen you looking so gorgeous as you did tonight;
I've never seen you shine so bright.
You were amazing.
I've never seen so many people want to be there by your side,
And when you turned to me and smiled,
It took my breath away.
I have never had such a feeling,
Such a feeling of complete and utter love
As I do tonight.

(To Chorus:)

LEAVING LAS VEGAS

Words and Music by
SHERYL CROW, BILL BOTTRELL, DAVID BAERWALD,
KEVIN GILBERT and DAVID RICKETTS

Verse:
Chorus:
Am7(4)
Dsus
D
G5
C2
G/B
G
re-call.
2. Oh, I'm bang-ing on my T. V. set,
and I check the odds and I,
and I place my bet.
I pour a drink and
I pull the blinds.
I won-der what I'll find.
I'm leav-ing Las Ve-
(Ve-) gas,
lights so bright,
palm sweat, black-
-jack on a Sat-ur-day night.
Leav-ing Las Ve - gas,

To Coda
1.
G5
C2
G/B
Am7(4)
Dsus
D
leav-ing for good,
for good.
I'm leav-ing for good.
D.S.
I'm leav-ing for good.
2.
To next strain
3.
D.S.
4.
D.S.S. al Coda
for good,
for
for good.
for good. Oh,
I'm leav-ing Las
Bridge:
Em
good.
I'm stand-ing in the
mid-dle of the des - ert,
wait-ing for my
G
ship to come in.
But now, no jok - er,

Verse 3:
Used to be I could drive up to Barstow for the night,
Find some crossroad trucker to demonstrate his might.
But these days it seems nowhere is far enough away,
So, I'm leaving Las Vegas today.
(To Chorus:)

Verse 4:
Quit my job as a dancer at the Lido des Girls,
Dealing blackjack until one or two.
Such a muddy line between the things you want
And the things you have to do.
(To Chorus:)

LITTLE DEUCE COUPE

Words by
ROGER CHRISTIAN

Music by
BRIAN WILSON

Medium Rock beat
Tacet
C
Well, I'm not brag - gin', babe, so don't put me down, but
lit - tle deuce coupe with a flat - head mill, but she'll
I've got the fast - est set of wheels in town.
walk a Thun - der - bird like it's stand - in' still.
F
When some - thing pulls up to me, it
She's port - ed and re - lieved, and she's

C
don't e - ven try. And if it had a set of wings, man, I know I could fly, she's my
stroked and she's bored. She'll do a hun-dred and for - ty with the top end floored, she's my
G
Dm
G7
C
lit - tle deuce coupe you don't know what I got.
lit - tle deuce coupe you don't know what I got.
1.
G7
2.
C7
F
Just a
She's got a com - pe - ti - tion clutch, with

C
four on the floor yeah, she purrs like a kit - ten till the lake pipes roar, and
F
D7
if that ain't e - nough to make you flip your wig, there's one more thing, I've got the
G7
C
pink slip, dad - dy! And com - in' off the line, when the lights turn green, she

F
3
blows 'em out - ta the wa - ter like you've nev - er seen. I get pushed out of shape, and it's
C
hard to steer, when I get rub - ber in a all four gears. She's my
G
Dm
G7
1.C
lit - tle deuce coupe, you don't know what I've got!
C7
2.C
C9+11
She's got a

(THE) LOGICAL SONG

Words and Music by
ROGER HODGSON and
RICK DAVIES

Ab
Adim
1., 3.
oh, play - ful - ly watch-ing me. But then they
oh, in - tel - lec - tu - al, cyn - i - cal.
2., 4.
Eb
Chorus
1. There are times
2. At night,
when all the world's a - sleep,
Am7b5/Eb
Ab/Eb
the ques - tions run too deep for such
Db
Fm/C
Bbm
Fm/Ab
a sim - ple man. Won't you please,

Eb
Am7b5/Eb
please tell me what we've learned?
I know
it sounds ab - surd
Ab/Eb
please tell me who I am.
Db
Fm/C
to Coda 2nd time
Bbm
Fm/Ab
"D.S. (3rd verse al coda"
I said,
Coda
Who I am,
who I am,

3rd Verse

I said, Now watch what you say or they'll be calling you a radical,
a liberal, oh, fanatical, criminal.
Oh, won't you sign up your name, we'd like to feel you're acceptable,
respectable, oh, presentable. A vegetable!

4th Verse

INSTRUMENTAL

(To 2nd Chorus)

LOOKS LIKE WE MADE IT

Words by
WILL JENNINGS

Music by
RICHARD KERR

Expressively
mp
C
F/C
C
There you are,
look - ing just the same as you did last time I touched you.
Love's so strange,
play - ing hide and seek with hearts and al - ways hurt - ing.
mp
F/C
C
And here I am,
close to get - tin' tan - gled up in - side the thought of you.
Do you
And we're the fools,
stand - ing close e - nough to touch those burn - ing mem - o - ries.
And if I

Am7
D11
D9
G
Am7
love him as much as I love her, and will that love be
hold you for the sake of all those times love made us lose our
D11
D7
G7
strong when old feel - ings start to stir? Looks like we
minds, could I ev - er let you go? Oh no we've
mp
C
G/C
F
G
made it, left each oth - er on the way to an - oth - er love.
mf
Em7
A7
Dm7
G11
C
G/C
Looks like we made it, or I

F
G
Em7
Am7
thought so till to - day, un - til you were there, ev - 'ry - where, and
1.
Dm
C/E
F
G11
C(add D)
C
G/C
F/C
all I could taste was love the way we made it.
decresc.
mp
2.
Dm
C/E
F
G11
Am
all I could taste was love the way we made it. Oh.
Em
Am
G11
(To D. S. Repeat and fade)
We made it. Looks like we

LOST IN YOUR EYES

Lyrics & Music by
TOM PETTY

Moderate rock ♩ = 88
N.C. G C/G
N.C. G C/G
N.C. G C/G
N.C. G C/G
mf
(with pedal)

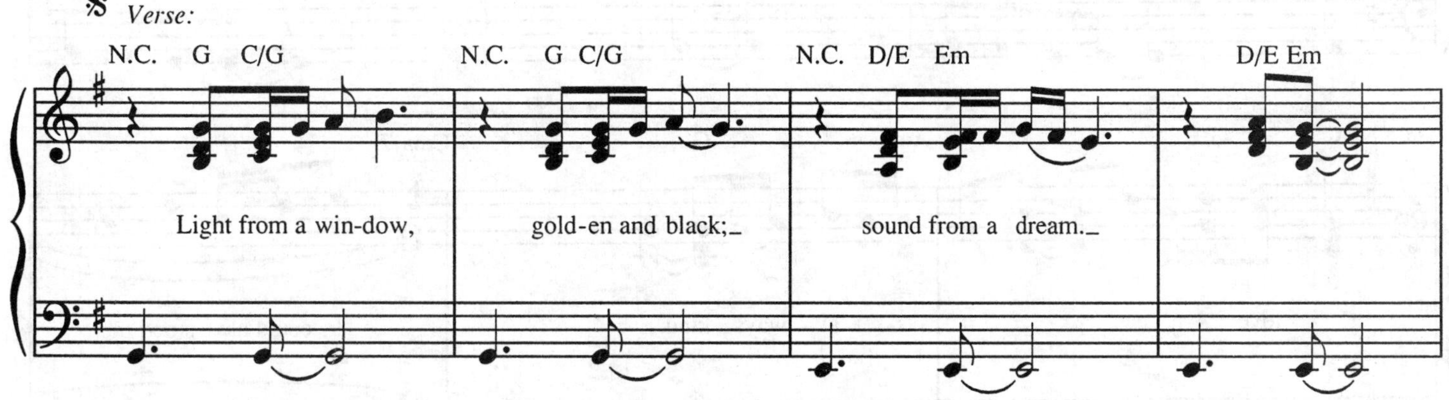
Verse:
N.C. G C/G
N.C. G C/G
N.C. D/E Em
D/E Em
Light from a win-dow,
gold-en and black;
sound from a dream.

N.C. G C/G
N.C. G C/G
N.C. D/E Em
I was hyp - no - tized,
I was par - a - lyzed.
I could hard-ly speak.

D/E Em
Am7
D
And
ba - by,
ba - by,

Am7
D
G/B
Chorus:
C
G/B
you nev - er re - al - ized that
I could have stood there
cresc.
f
Am7
G
C
G/B
Am7
G
lost in your eyes.
Stood there wait-ing and not re - al - ized
C
G/B
Am7
G
Cmaj7
love is-n't eas - y, it is-n't al - ways kind.
I could have stood there
To Coda
1.
D.S.
N.C.
G
C/G
lost in your eyes.
2.
Bridge:
G
D
C
And though, some - times I won - der, yes, I won - der, I real-ly, real-ly

Verse 2:
Guess I understand it, guess I sort of have to,
Guess I kind of see.
Just because it could have been, doesn't mean it had to ever mean a thing.
And baby, baby, I could say it all the time, that . . .
(To Chorus:)

Verse 3:
Guess I understand it, guess I sort of have to,
Guess I kind of see.
Just because it could have been, doesn't mean it had to ever mean a thing.
And baby, baby, you never realized that . . .
(To Chorus:)

LOVE THE ONE YOU'RE WITH

Words and Music by
STEPHEN STILLS

C
F/C bass
C
Am
is so far a - way.
for something to do.
any more ad - vice.
Well, there's a rose
G
F
Am
G
in the fist-ed glove
and the ea-gle flies
with the
F
Am
G
F
dove,
and if you can't be
with the one you love hon-ey,
C
F/C bass
C
F/C bass
Love The One You're With,
Love The One You're With,
F
C
F/C bass
1.
C
F/C bass
Love The One You're With,
Love The One You're With.

2. and Fine
Bb/ C bass
F/ C bass
C
F
C7
dit dit dit dit dit dit dit dit,
dit dit dit. dit dit dit.
Fine
Love The One You're With,
3. Turn your heart-
D.S. al Fine

MANEATER

Words by SARA ALLEN,
DARYL HALL and JOHN OATES

Music by
DARYL HALL and JOHN OATES

D
A/C#
C
many have paid to see what you think you're getting for free the woman is wild, a she-cat tamed by the
wouldn't if I were you I know what she can do, she's deadly man she could really
B
Em7
A
A#dim
purr of a jaguar. Money's the matter. If you're in it for love, you ain't gonna get too
rip your world apart. Mind over matter oo the beauty is there, but a beast is in the
Bm
A/B
B
Bm
A
G
far.
heart.
Oh, here she comes, watch out boy, she'll chew you up. Oh, here she comes, she's a Man-
F#
Bm
A
Em7
eater. Oh, here she comes, watch out boy, she'll chew you up. Oh, here she comes, she a Man-
G
A
Bm
Bm
Bm
A
eater. (Synth) I (Sax solo) (echo)

G
A
Bm
A
G
A
Bm
A
G
A
Bm
A
Em7
F#7
Bm
A
G
F#
Oh, here she comes, watch out boy, she'll chew you up. Oh, here she comes, she's a Man - eat - er.
Bm
A
Em7
G
A
Repeat and Fade
Oh, here she comes, watch out boy, she'll chew you up. Oh, here she comes, she's a Man - eat - er.

MORE THAN WORDS

Lyrics and Music by
BETTENCOURT, CHERONE

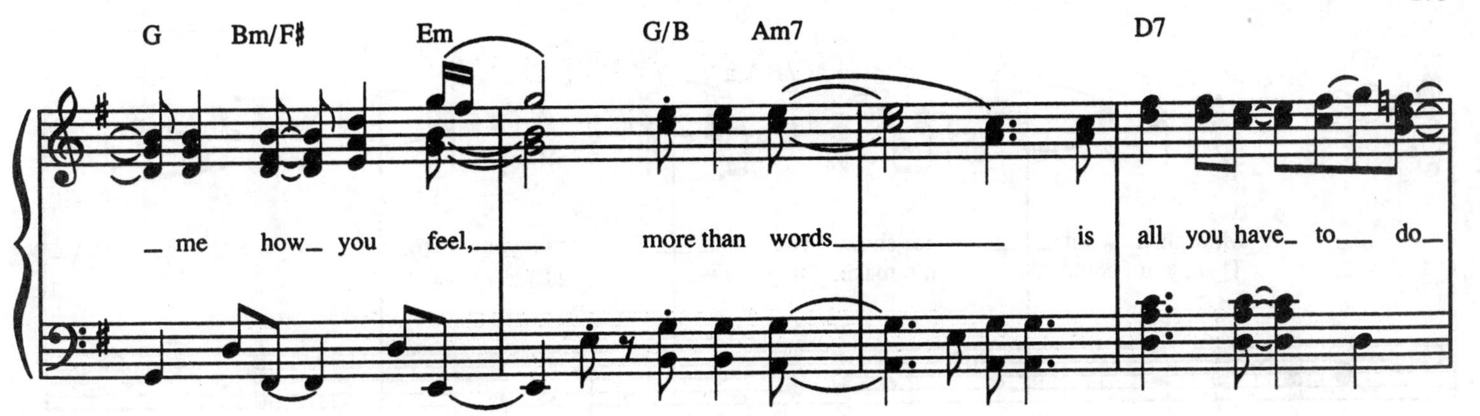
G Bm/F♯ Em G/B Am7 D7
_ me how_ you feel,___ more than words___ is all you have_ to_ do_

G7 G7/B C Cm G Em7
_ to make_ it_ real.___ Then, you would - n't have_ to say___ that you love_

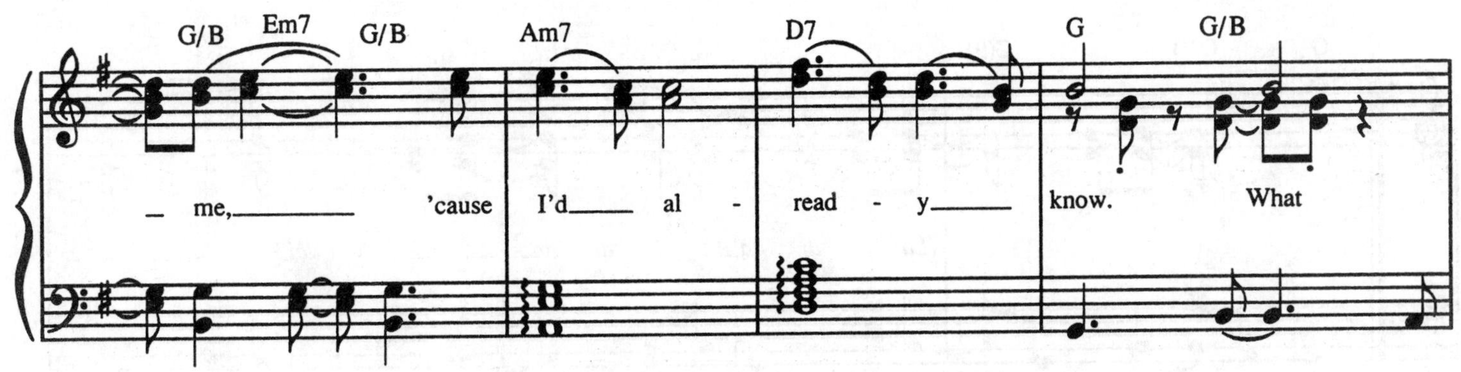
G/B Em7 G/B Am7 D7 G G/B
_ me,___ 'cause I'd___ al - read - y___ know. What

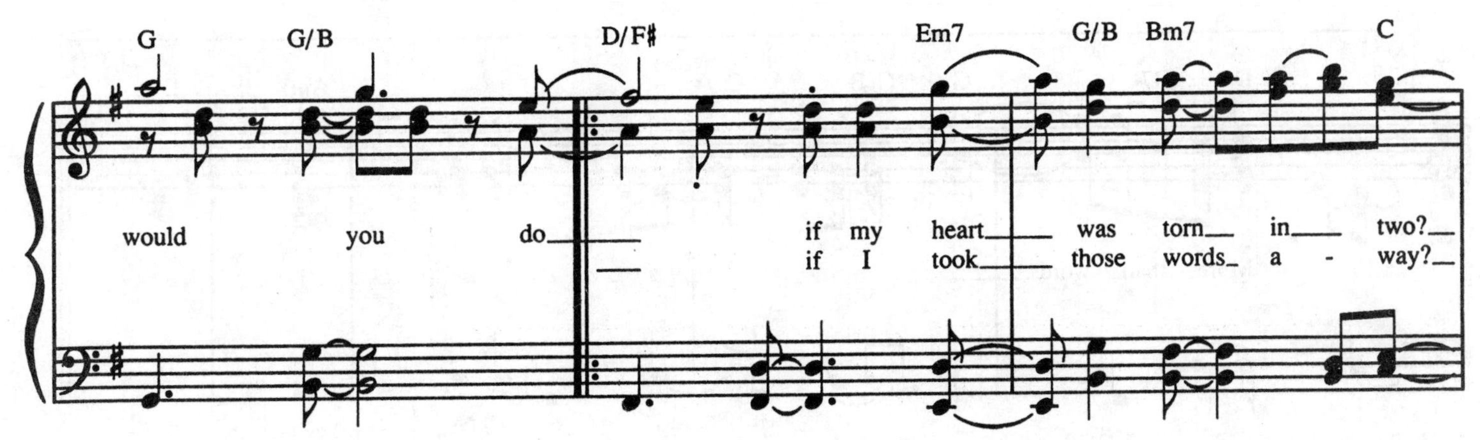
G G/B D/F♯ Em7 G/B Bm7 C
would you do___ if my heart___ was torn_ in___ two?_
___ if I took___ those words_ a - way?_

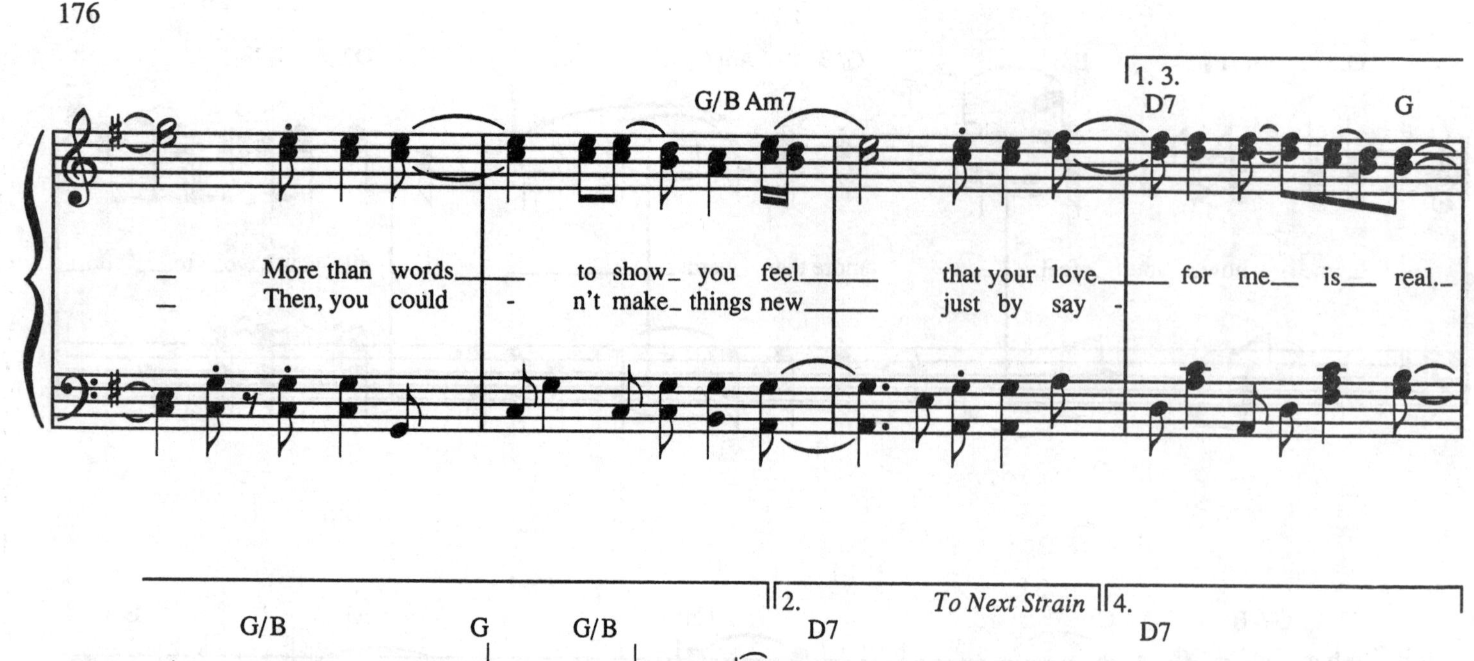
G/B Am7
1. 3.
D7
G
More than words to show you feel that your love for me is real.
Then, you could - n't make things new just by say -

G/B
G
G/B
2.
To Next Strain
4.
D7
D7
What would you say - in' "I love you." - in' "I love you."

G
G/B
C(9)
G/B
Am7
G/B
C
(La di da da di da di dai dai da.

1.
D.S. 𝄋
D
D7
G
G/B
C(9)
Am7
D7
) More than words. La di da da di da.)

Verse 2:
Now that I have tried to talk to you
And make you understand.
All you have to do is close your eyes
And just reach out your hands.
And touch me, hold me close, don't ever let me go.
More than words is all I ever needed you to show.
Then you wouldn't have to say
That you love me 'cause I'd already know.
(To Chorus:)

NEVER BEEN TO SPAIN

Words and Music by
HOYT AXTON

Rock Blues Feel
G
C
1. Well I Nev - er Been To Spain
4. (instrumental ad lib.)
but I kind-a like the
mf
G
C
C
(G bass)
mu - sic.
I hear the la-dies are in - sane_ there
and they sure know how to
G
D
use it.
They don't a - buse it.
They'll nev - er
C
G
lose it.
I can't re - fuse it.
2. Well, I Nev - er Been To
(fade out)

C
C (G bass)
G
Eng - land, But I kind - a like the Bea - tles.
Heav - en, but I've been to O - kla - ho - ma.
C
C (G bass)
G
Oh, I head - ed for Las Ve-gas on - ly made it out to Need - les.
Oh, they tell me I was born there, but I real - ly don't re - mem - ber.
D
1. C
G
Can you feel it? It must be real it feels so good, feels so
In O - kla - ho - ma, Not A - ri -
2. C
G
C
G
(D.S. to fade)
good. 3. Well I Nev - er Been To -zo - na. What does it mat - ter? What does it mat - ter?

NOWHERE TO GO

Words and Music by
MELISSA ETHERIDGE

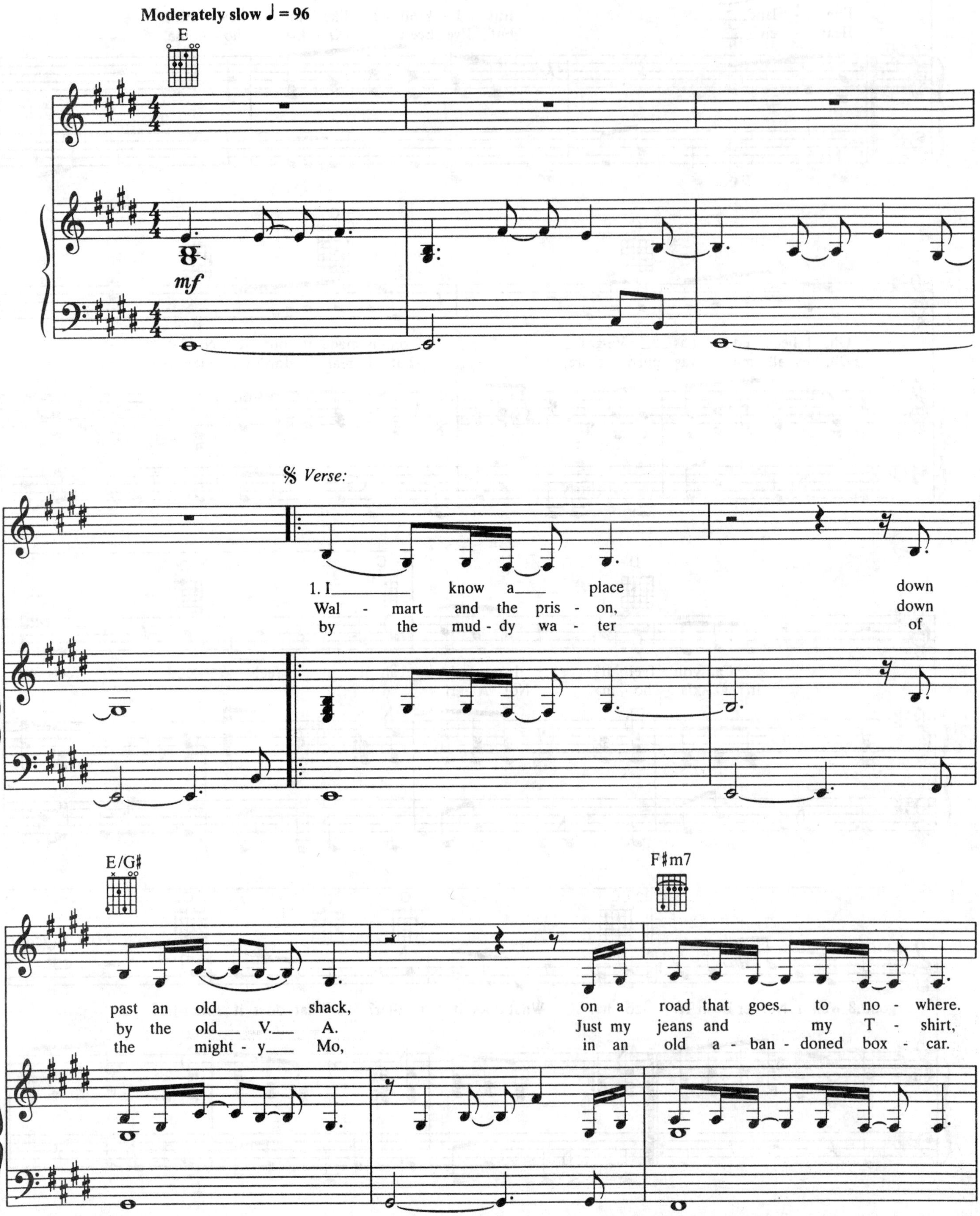

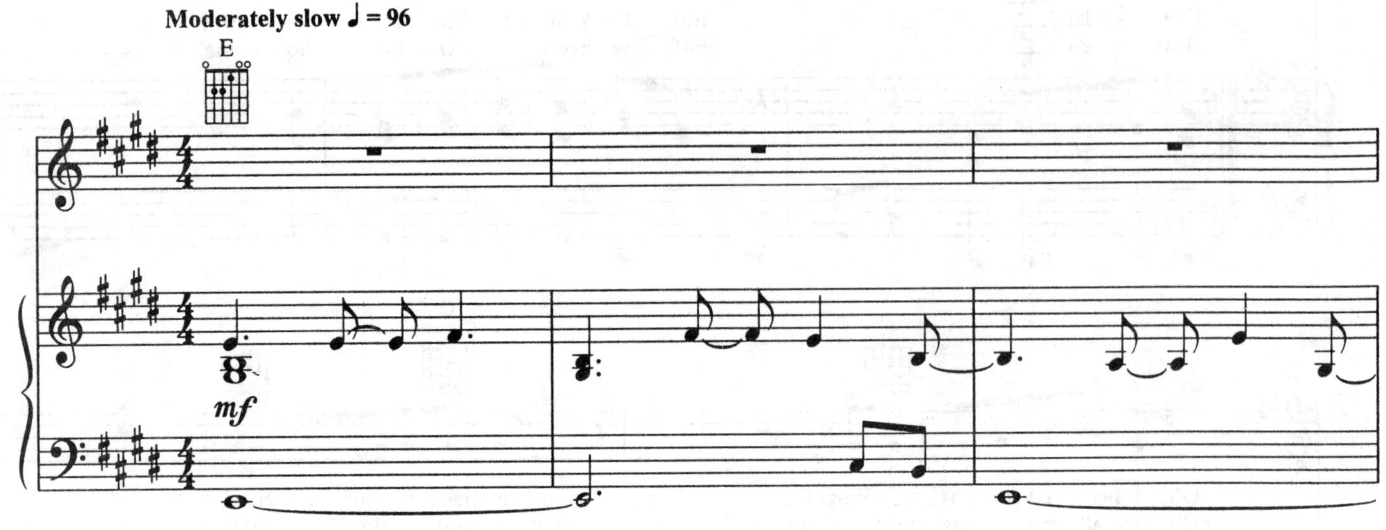

Moderately slow ♩ = 96
E
mf
Verse:
1. I know a place down
Wal - mart and the pris - on, down
by the mud - dy wa - ter of
E/G♯
F♯m7
past an old shack, on a road that goes to no - where.
by the old V. A. Just my jeans and my T - shirt,
the might - y Mo, in an old a - ban - doned box - car.

A(9)
Ain't_ no - bod - y com - ing back. We can
and_ my blue Chev - ro - let. It's
Will_ I ev - er know? Dance with
E
E/G♯
go_ there_ to - night, we_ can talk un - til_ dawn,_
Sat - ur - day_ night, feels_ like ev - ery - thing's_ wrong._
me_ for - ev - er. This mo - ment_ is_ di - vine._
F♯m7
or may - be_ some - thing_ else. I'll leave the_
I've got some straw - ber - ry_ wine, I want to_
I'm so close_ to_ heav - en, this_
A(9)
Bsus
A(9)
ra - di - o_ on,_ the ra - di - o_ on._
get you_ a - lone,_ get you_ a - lone._
hell is_ not_ mine,_ this hell is_ not_ mine._

Chorus:
B
Bsus
E
There's no one to hear. You
A(9)
E
might as well scream. They nev - er woke up
A(9)
from the A - mer - i - can dream. And they
E
F♯m7
E/G♯
don't un - der - stand what they don't see. And they look through you, and they look

F♯m7
E
E/G♯
past me.
Oh,
you and I danc - ing slow,
F♯m7
1.
A(9)
E
and we got no - where to go.
2.3.
A(9)
2. Past the got no - where to go.
E
F♯m7
E/G♯
A(9)

E
F♯m7
To Coda
E/G♯
A(9)
E
D.S. 𝄋 al Coda
3. Down
Coda
E/G♯
A(9)
E
We got no - where_ to go.
F♯m7
E/G♯
A(9)
Repeat ad lib. and fade
We got no - where_ to go._

ROCK WITH YOU

Words and Music by
ROD TEMPERTON

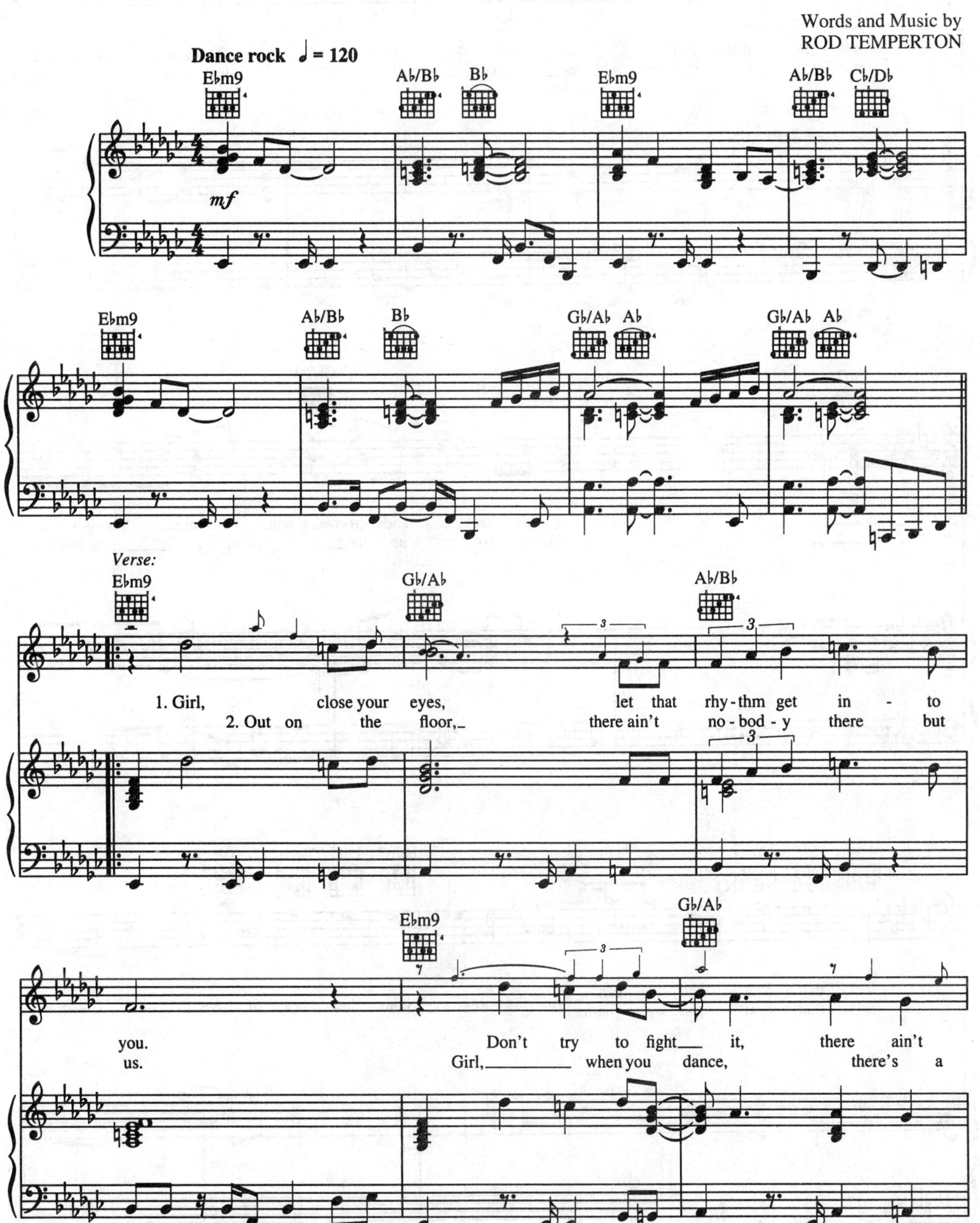
Dance rock ♩ = 120
Ebm9 Ab/Bb Bb Ebm9 Ab/Bb Cb/Db
mf
Ebm9 Ab/Bb Bb Gb/Ab Ab Gb/Ab Ab
Verse:
Ebm9 Gb/Ab Ab/Bb
1. Girl, close your eyes, let that rhy-thm get in - to
2. Out on the floor, there ain't no - bod - y there but
Ebm9 Gb/Ab
you. Don't try to fight it, there ain't
us. Girl, when you dance, there's a

Ab/Bb
Gbmaj7
noth - in' that you can do.
mag - ic that must be love.
Re - lax your mind,
Just take it slow,
Fm7
Cbmaj7
Gb/Ab
lay back and groove with mine. You got - ta
'cause we got so far to go. When you
Ebm7
Fm7
Gbmaj7
N.C.
Ab
feel that heat and we can
feel that heat and we're gon-na
ride the boo-gie. Share that beat of love. I wan-na

Chorus:
Ebm9
Ab/Bb
Bb
Ebm9
Ab/Bb
Cb/Db
rock with you.
(All night.)
Dance you in - to day.
(Sun - light.)
I wan-na
Ebm9
Ab/Bb
Bb
Gb/Ab
Ab
1.
Gb/Ab
Ab
rock with you.
(All night.)
We're gon-na rock the night a - way.
2.
Gb/Ab
Ab
Bridge:
Bbm
And when the groove is dead and gone,
Eb9
Gbmaj7
yeah,
you know that love sur-vives,

Db/F Cbmaj7 Gb/Ab Ab

— so we can rock for - ev - er___

Ebm9 Ab/Bb Bb

on. *(First time only)*

Ebm9 Ab/Bb Cb/Db Ebm9

Ab/Bb Bb/C Cb/Db

1.

I wan - na rock with you. I wan - na groove with you.

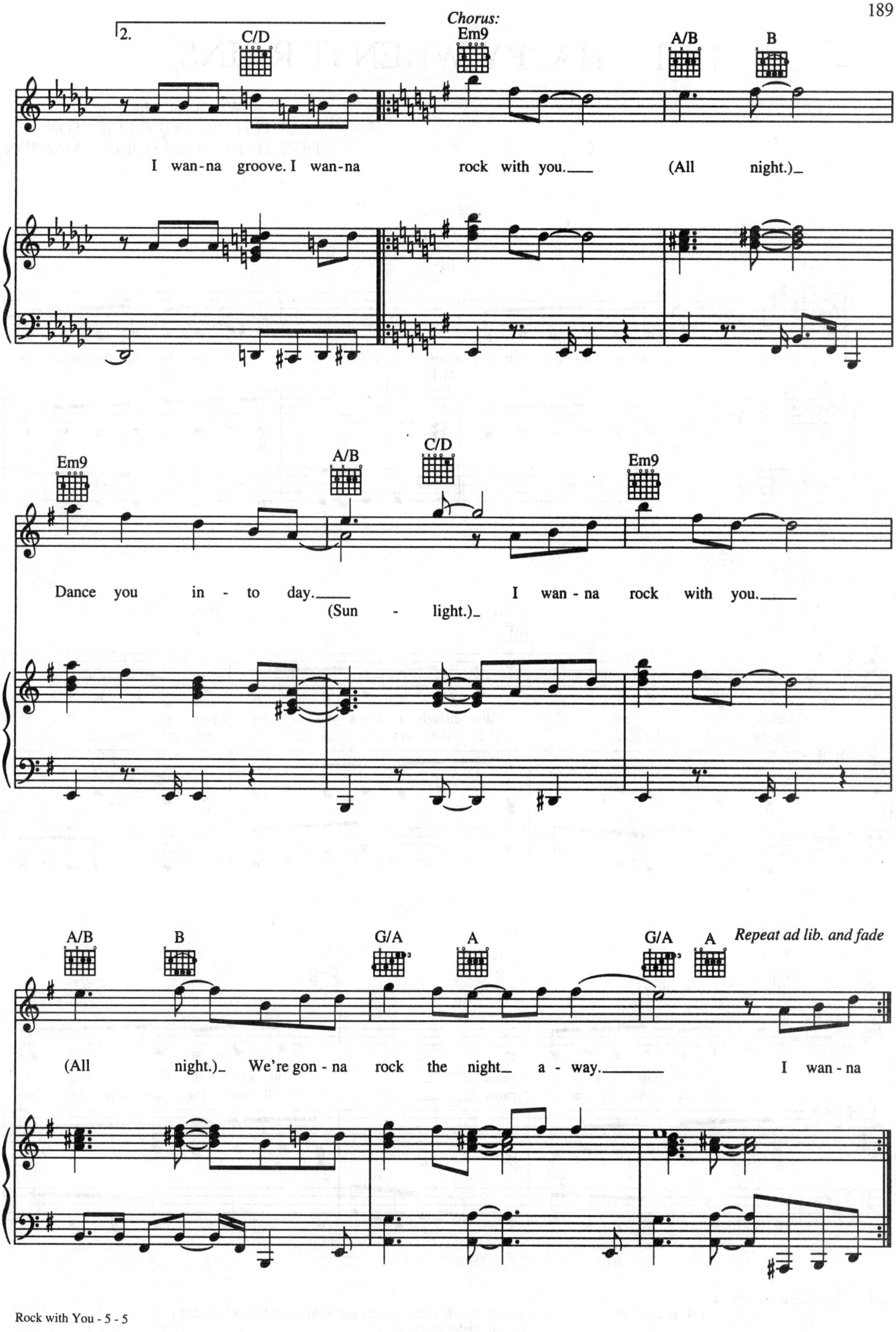

2.

C/D

Chorus:

Em9 A/B B

I wan-na groove. I wan-na rock with you.___ (All night.)_

Em9 A/B C/D Em9

Dance you in - to day.___ I wan - na rock with you.___

(Sun - light.)_

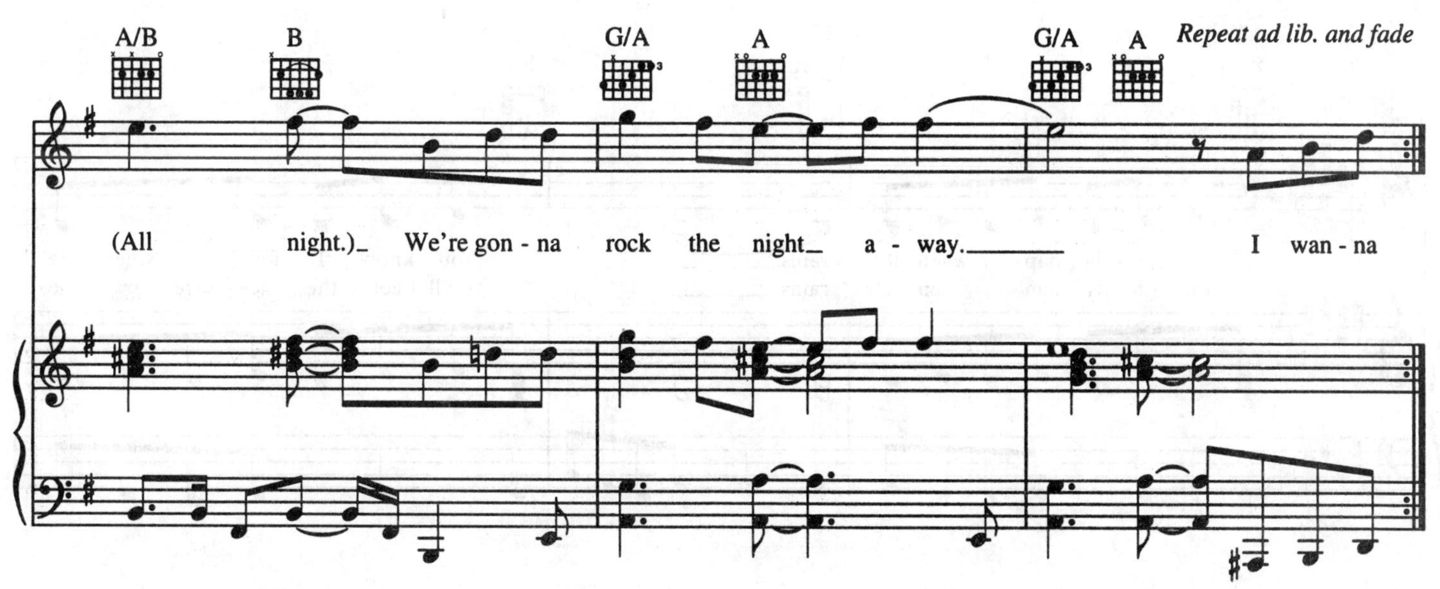

ONLY HAPPY WHEN IT RAINS

Words and Music by
BUTCH VIG, DOUG ERICKSON,
STEVE MARKER and SHIRLEY MANSON

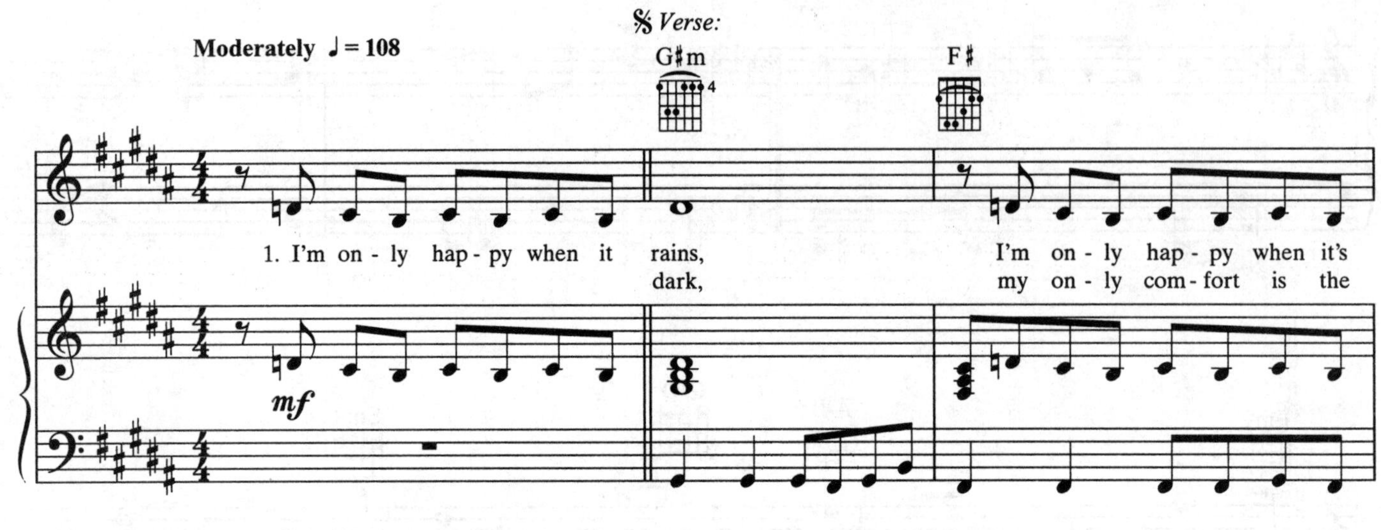

E
C♯m
E
news is bad,
and why it feels so good to
feel so bad,
time I'm through,
when I com-plain a-bout
me and you,

F♯
B
I'm on-ly hap-py when it
rains.
I'm on-ly hap-py when it
rains.

Chorus:
C♯
G♯m
A
Pour your mis-er-y down,
pour your

B
C♯
G♯m
mis - er - y down on me. Pour your mis - er - y down,
A
B
To Coda
F♯
pour your mis - er - y down on me.
Verse:
N.C.
G♯m
F♯
2. I'm on - ly hap - py when it rains, I feel good when things are
E
C♯m
E
go - ing wrong, I on - ly lis - ten to the sad, sad songs,

F♯
B
I'm on - ly hap - py when it rains.
C♯
G♯m
A
B
C♯
G♯m
A
B
N.C.
D.S. 𝄋 al Coda
3. I on - ly smile in the

Coda
C♯
G♯m
A
me. Pour your mis - er - y down, pour your
B
C♯
G♯m
mis - er - y down on me, pour your mis - er - y down.
A
B
You can keep me com - pa - ny as long as you don't care.
Verse:
F♯
N.C.
G♯m
4. I'm on - ly hap - py when it rains,

F♯
E
C♯m
you wan - na hear a - bout my new ob - ses - sion, I'm rid - ing high up - on a
E
F♯
G♯m
deep de - pres - sion, I'm on - ly hap - py when it rains.
(Pour some
E
C♯m
mis - er - y down on me.)
I'm on - ly hap - py when it
G♯m
E
C♯m
Repeat ad lib. and fade
rains.
(Pour some mis - er - y down on me.)
I'm on - ly hap - py when it

RAINY DAYS AND MONDAYS

Lyrics by
PAUL WILLIAMS

Music by
ROGER NICHOLS

Am7
(Dbass)
G/B
Am7
C/D
no - thing to do but frown;
some kind of lone-ly clown;
no - thing to do but frown;
Rain-y Days And Mon-days al - ways get me
Rain-y Days And Mon-days al - ways get me
Rain-y Days And Mon-days al - ways get me
G/D
D7sus4
1.
G/D
D7sus4
2. 3.
G/D
D
B7/D♯
down.
down.
down.
Em7
Cmaj7
Am7
D7
Gmaj7
Fun-ny but it seems I al - ways wind up here with you,
Bm7
Cmaj7
D7sus4/A
D7
B7/D♯
Em7
Cmaj7
nice to know some-bo-dy loves me.
Fun-ny but it seems that it's the

Am7
D7
Bm7
Bm7
Cmaj7
on - ly thing to do,
run and find the one who
To Coda
D. S. al Coda
Coda
D7sus4/A
D
D7sus4/A
D
E7sus4/B
E7sus4
E7
loves me.
A
C♯m/G♯
C♯m7(-5)/G
F♯7
What I feel has come and gone be - fore,
Bm11
C♯m7
Bm11/D
C♯m7
No need to talk it out,
We know what it's all a - bout

F♯m7 (E bass) Dmaj7 (C♯bass) Bm7 (E bass) A/C♯
Hang-in' a-round noth-in' to do but frown.
1.
Bm7 D/E Amaj7/E D/E C♯7/E♯
Rain-y Days And Mon-days al-ways get me down.
2.
D Bm7 C♯m D/E
Rain-y Days And Mon-days al - ways get me
A/E Bm7/E A/E Bm7/E A/E Bm7/E A9sus4/E Amaj7
down.

REFUGEE

Words and Music by
TOM PETTY and
MICHAEL CAMPBELL

Moderately (♩ = 120)
F♯m
A
E
Play 4 times
mf
F♯m
A
E
(1) We got some-thin', we both know it, we don't talk too much a - bout
Verse 2.,3. - See additional lyrics
p
F♯m
A
E
F♯m
it.
Ain't no real big se - cret,
A
E
F♯m
A
E
all the same, some-how, we get a - round it.
Lis-ten,

Chorus:
D
it don't real - ly mat - ter to me, ba - by,
Chorus 2. 3. - See additional lyrics
mf
B7
you be - lieve what you want to be - lieve, you see, you
F#m
A
E
F#m
A
don't have to live like a ref - u - gee.
f
1.
E
2.3.
E
F#m
A
No ba-by, you don't have to

To Coda
E
F#m
A
E
live like a ref - u - gee.
A
Ba - by, we ain't the first.
I'm sure a lot of oth - er
D
lov - ers been burned.
Right now this seems real to you, but it's
E
D.C. al Coda
one of those things you got - ta feel to be true.

Coda

E F♯m A E

Ba-by, you don't ___ have ___ to live like a ref-u-gee.

Repeat ad lib & Fade

F♯m A E F♯m A E

(instr. solo ad lib)

(Additional Lyrics)

Verse 2:	Somewhere, somehow, somebody must have kicked you around some. Tell me why you want to lay there, revel in your abandon. Honey,
Chorus 2:	It don't make no difference to me, baby, Everybody's had to fight to be free, you see, You don't have to live like a refugee. (to 2nd ending)
Verse 3:	Somewhere, somehow, somebody must have kicked you around some. Who knows ? Maybe you were kidnapped, tied up, taken away, and held for ransom. Honey,
Chorus 3:	It don't really matter to me, baby, Everybody's had to fight to be free, you see, You don't have to live like a refugee. (to 3rd ending)

RISE

Words and Music by
ANDY ARMER and
RANDY BADAZZ

Medium Funky Tempo

Gbmaj7
Cbmaj7
pass us by, not let life seem so shy.
un - der - stand, reach out a help - ing hand.
all our plans and find what peace we can.
Cbmaj7 (Bbbass)
Abm7
If you just be - lieve, you will re - al -
If you just be - lieve we are what we
If you just be - lieve. you will re - al -
Gb
E
ize, you will sense it's time
seem, hid - ing from our - selves,
ize, you will sense it's time

To Coda
1.
2.
Eb
Gm7
C7(#5)
we've all got to rise. We all need to
hid - ing from our dreams.
we've all got to rise.
Eb
Bbm7(Ebbass)
Eb7
Abmaj7
Rise and shine reach up for the
G11
C7(#9)
C7(b9)(#5)
Abmaj7
sky, let your life
G11
Ab(C bass)
Ebm7
Ab7(b9)(b5)
live in-side your mind. Fly a

D♭maj9
Cm7
way
and
find
who you
F13 (♯11)
F♯m9
are,
and just
find
your own
D.S. al Coda
B13
Emaj9
A7 (♭5)
Gm7
C7 (♯5)
star
and
shine.
We've all
got
to
Coda
Gm7
C7 (♯5)
F7
Repeat & fade

RUN-AROUND

Moderately fast ♩ = 150

By JOHN POPPER

Am
D
G
C
Am
D
1. Oh
Verse:
G
C
Am
D
G
C
once up - on a mid - night dea - rie I woke with some-thing in my head.
2.3. See additional lyrics
Am
D
G
C
Am
D
I could-n't es - cape the mem - o - ry of a phone
G
C
Am
D
G
C
call and of what you said. Like a game show con - tes - tant with a

Am
D
G
C
part - ing gift__ I could not____ be - lieve__ my___ eyes,___ when I saw__
__ through the voice_ of a trust - ed friend_ who needs to hu - mor me and__ tell me
lies.__ Yeah,_ hu - mor me and__ tell me lies. And
Pre-Chorus:
I'll lie too and say I______ don't mind,_____ and as we seek,_ so shall_

Am
D
G
C
Am
D
we find. And when you're feel-ing op-en I'll still be here, but
G
C
Am
D
G
C
not with-out a cer-tain de-gree of fear of what will be, with
Am
D
G
C
Am
D
you and me. I still can see things hope-ful-ly. But you,
Chorus:
G
C
Am
D
G
C
why you wan-na give me a run-a-round?

Am
D
G
C
To Coda
Is it a sure fire way to speed things up, when
all it does is slow me down?
1.
down?
2.
(Harmonica solo)
3

G C Am D

G C Am D

G C Am D

G C Am D

G
C
Am
D
D.S. 𝄋 al Coda
Tra - la - la
Coda
all it does is slow me down? Oh, you,
why you wan-na give me the run - a - round? Is it a sure
fire way to speed things up, when all it does is slow

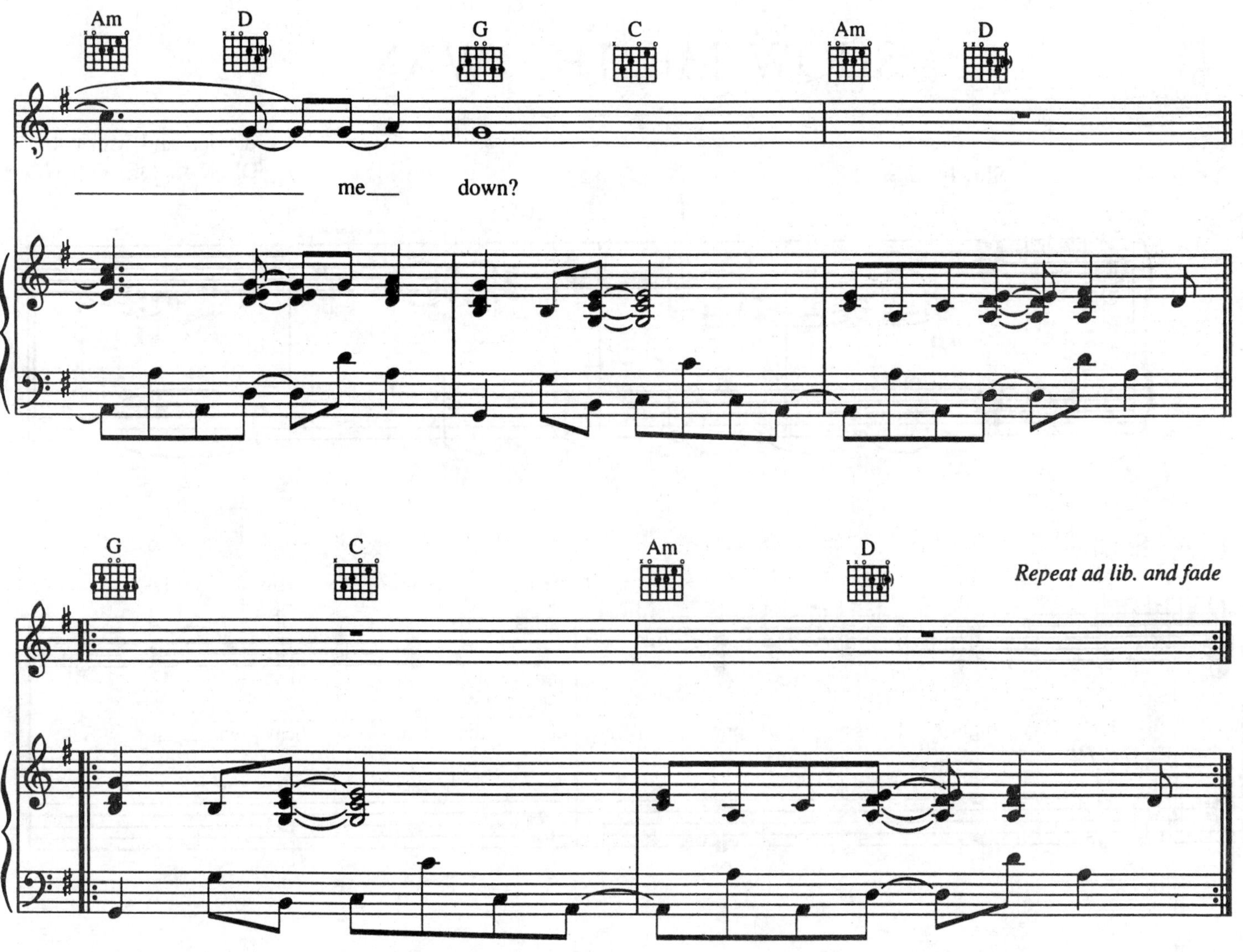

Verse 2:
And shake me and my confidence
About a great many things.
But I've been there, I can see it cower
Like a nervous magician waiting in the wings.
Of a bad play where the heroes are right,
And nobody thinks or expects too much,
And Hollywood's calling for the movie rights,
Singing, "Hey babe, let's keep in touch,
Hey baby, let's keep in touch."

Pre-Chorus:
But I want more than a touch,
I want you to reach me,
And show me all the things no one else can see.
So what you feel becomes mine as well,
And soon if we're lucky we'd be unable to tell
What's yours and mine, the fishing's fine,
And it doesn't have to rhyme, so don't you
Feed me a line.
(To Chorus:)

Verse 3:
Tra-lala bomba, dear this is the pilot speaking
And I've got some news for you.
It seems my ship still stands no matter what you drop,
And there ain't a whole lot that you can do.
Oh sure, the banner may be torn
And the wind's gotten colder and perhaps I've grown a little cynical,
But I know no matter what the waitress brings
I shall drink in and always be full
My cup shall always be full.

Pre-Chorus:
Oh, I like coffee and I like tea,
I'd like to be able to enter a final plea,
I still got this dream that you just can't shake.
I love you to the point you can no longer take.
Well alright, okay, so be that way.
I hope and pray that there's something left to say.
(To Chorus:)

SHOW ME THE WAY

Lyrics and Music by
DENNIS DE YOUNG

Gb Abm7 Db/F Ebm Cb Dbsus Db
feel this emp - ty place in - side; so a - fraid that I've lost my faith. Show me the
mf
Chorus:
Gb Db Cb Gb Db Cb
way, show me the way.
Take me to -
Bring me to -
f
To Coda
Gb Db/F Ebm7 Gb/Db Abm7 Dbsus Db
night to the riv - er and wash my il - lu - sions a - way.
night to the moun-tain and take my con - fu - sion a - way.
Please show me the
1.
D.S.
2.
Gb Cb/Gb Db/Gb Cb/Gb Gb Cb/Gb Db/Gb Cb/Gb Gb Cb/Gb Db/Gb Cb
way.
2. And
Bridge:
Bb Ebm
and if I see a light, should I be - lieve? Tell me, how will I

A♭7
A♭m7
D♭sus
D♭
D♭sus
D♭
A
B/A Amaj7
B/A
know?
A
B/A
A
B/A
Amaj7
B/A
D♭
C♭/D♭
D♭
C♭/D♭
D.S.S. 𝄋𝄋 al Coda
Show me the
Coda
G♭
D♭
C♭
G♭
D♭
C♭
way,
show me the
way.
Take me
to -
G♭
D♭/F
E♭m7
G♭/D♭
A♭m7
D♭sus
D♭
night
to the riv - er
and wash my
il - lu - sions a -
way.
Show
me the
G♭
D♭
C♭
G♭
D♭
C♭
way,
show
me the
way.
Give
me
the

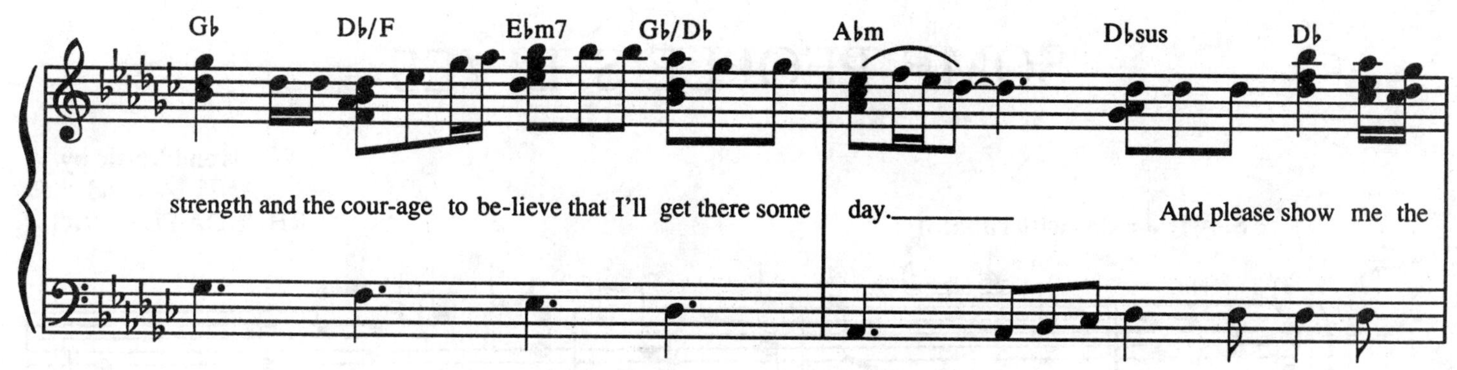
G♭ D♭/F E♭m7 G♭/D♭ A♭m D♭sus D♭
strength and the cour-age to be-lieve that I'll get there some day.
And please show me the

G♭ C♭/G♭ D♭/G♭ C♭/G♭ G♭ C♭/G♭ D♭/G♭ C♭/G♭ G♭ C♭/G♭ G♭ D♭/G♭
way.
mf
mp Slower
G A♭m7 D♭/F G♭ E♭m C♭maj7 D♭sus D♭
p
Ev - 'ry night I say a pray'r in the hopes that there's a heav-en.

Verse 2:
And as I slowly drift to sleep
For a moment dreams are sacred.
I close my eyes and know there's peace
In a world so filled with hatred.
Then I wake up each morning and turn on the news
To find we've so far to go.
And I keep on hoping for a sign
So afraid I just won't know.
(To Chorus:)

SOME PEOPLE'S LIVES

Words and Music by
JANIS IAN and
RHONDA FLEMING

Slowly ♩ = 88 (with rubato)

N.C.

mp

with pedal

C Gm7

Some peo - ple's lives___ run down like clocks.___

mf

C
Gm7
Am
Some lives wear out like old ten-nis shoes no one can
Gsus G Am/G G
F
Gsus G
use. Well, it's sad but it's true. Did-n't an-y-bod-y tell them?
F
G
F
Am/G G
Dm7
Did-n't an-y-bod-y see? Did-n't an-y-bod-y love them like you love

G
C
Gm7
me? Some peo-ple's eyes fade like their dreams, too
Am
Gsus G Am/G G C/G G7
C
tired to rise, too tired to sleep. Some peo-ple
Gm7
Am
Gsus
laugh when they need to cry, and they nev - er know
G
F
G
F
why. Did-n't an - y - bod - y tell them that's not how it has to

G F Am/G G Dm7 G Dm6/F
be? Did-n't an-y-bod-y love them like you love me?
E E7/G♯ Asus4/2 Am E/A Am Asus4/2 Am7 D Em7
Some peo-ple ask if the tears have to fall. Then why take your chanc-
D7/F♯ Gsus4/2 G Am/G G C/G G7 C
-es? Why both-er at all? And some peo-ple's lives are as
rit.
a tempo
Gm7 Am Gsus4/2
cold as their lips, they just need to be
rit.

G F Am/G G F
kissed. Does-n't an - y - bod - y tell___ them? Does-n't an - y - bod - y
a tempo
a tempo
G F Am/G G Dm/F E E7(♯9) G♯dim7
3
see? Does-n't an - y - bod - y love___them like you love
Am Em/G F C/E Dm7 F/G G7 C Dm/C C Dm/C F/C
me? 'Cuz that's all they need.
rit.
a tempo
rit.
a tempo
C N.C.
rit.
8vb

STUPID GIRL

Words and Music by
DOUG ERICKSON, SHIRLEY MANSON, STEVE MARKER,
BUTCH VIG, MICK JONES and JOE STRUMMER

Stupid Girl - 5 - 1

F♯5
B5
is what you get.
𝄋 Bridge:
D♯m
G♯2
D♯m
Don't be - lieve in fear,
Don't be - lieve in love,
Don't be - lieve in fear,
don't be - lieve in faith.
don't be - lieve in hate.
don't be - lieve in pain.
G♯2
D♯m
G♯2
Don't be - lieve in an - y - thing
Don't be - lieve in an - y - thing
Don't be - lieve in an - y - thing
Chorus:
D♯m
B
F♯7
that you can't break.
that you can't waste.
that you can't tame.
1.3. You stu - pid girl.
2. You stu - pid girl.

B
F#7
B
You stu - pid girl.
You stu - pid girl.
F#7
B
F#7
To Coda
All you had you wast - ed,
Can't be - lieve you fake it,
all you had you wast -
can't be - lieve you fake
B
F#7
B
- ed.
it.
F#7
B
F#7

B
F♯7
1.
B
2.
B
F♯7
B
F♯7
1.
B
2.
D.S. 𝄋 al Coda
B
Coda
B
F♯7
- ed.
1.2. You stu - pid girl.
3. (Inst. solo ad lib....

Verse 2:
What drives you on can drive you mad.
A million lies to sell yourself is all you ever had.
(To Bridge:)

A SONG FOR YOU

Lyrics and Music by
LEON RUSSELL

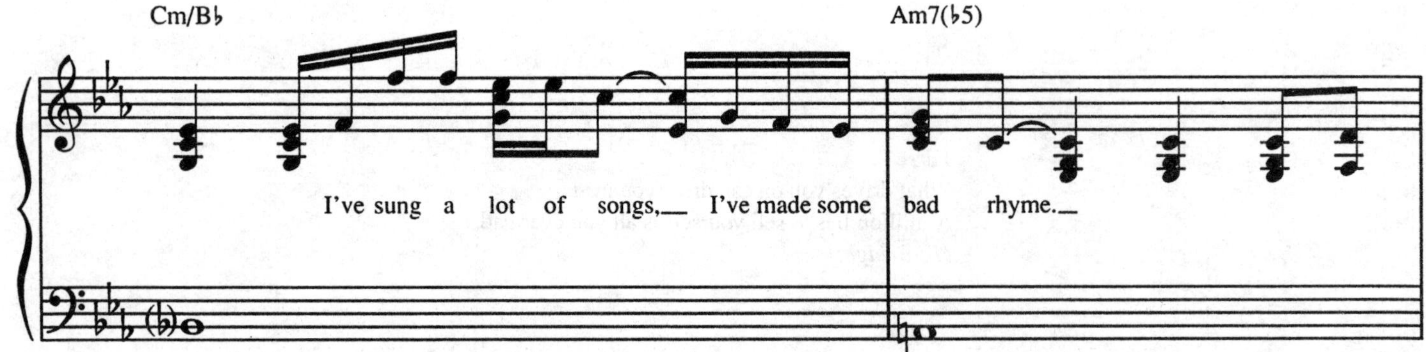

Ab
Eb/G
Fm7
Eb/G
I've act-ed out my life in stag-es
with ten thou-sand peo-ple watch-ing,
Ab
Eb/Bb
Ab/Bb
Eb
G7
but we're a-lone and I'm just a-sing-ing
this song for you.
Cm
3
G7/B
I know your im-age of me is what I
hope to be.
Ba-by,
Cm/Bb
Am7(b5)
I treat-ed you un-kind-ly, but
girl, can't you see
Ab
Eb/G
Fm7
Eb/G
there's no one more im-por-tant to me?
So dar-ling, can't you please see through me?

A♭ E♭/B♭ A♭/B♭ E♭ G7
'Cause we're a - lone now, and I'm singing my song for you.
Cm G7/B E♭/B♭ Am7(♭5)
You taught me pre-cious se-crets of the truth, with-hold - ing noth-ing.
A♭ E♭/B♭ A♭/B♭ A♭/E♭ E♭ G7/D
You came out in front and I was hid - ing.
cresc.
Cm G7/B E♭/B♭ Am7(♭5)
But now, I'm so much bet-ter, so if my words don't come to-geth-er,
f
A♭ E♭/G F7 A♭/B♭ B♭7
lis-ten to the mel - o - dy, 'cause my love's in there hid - ing.

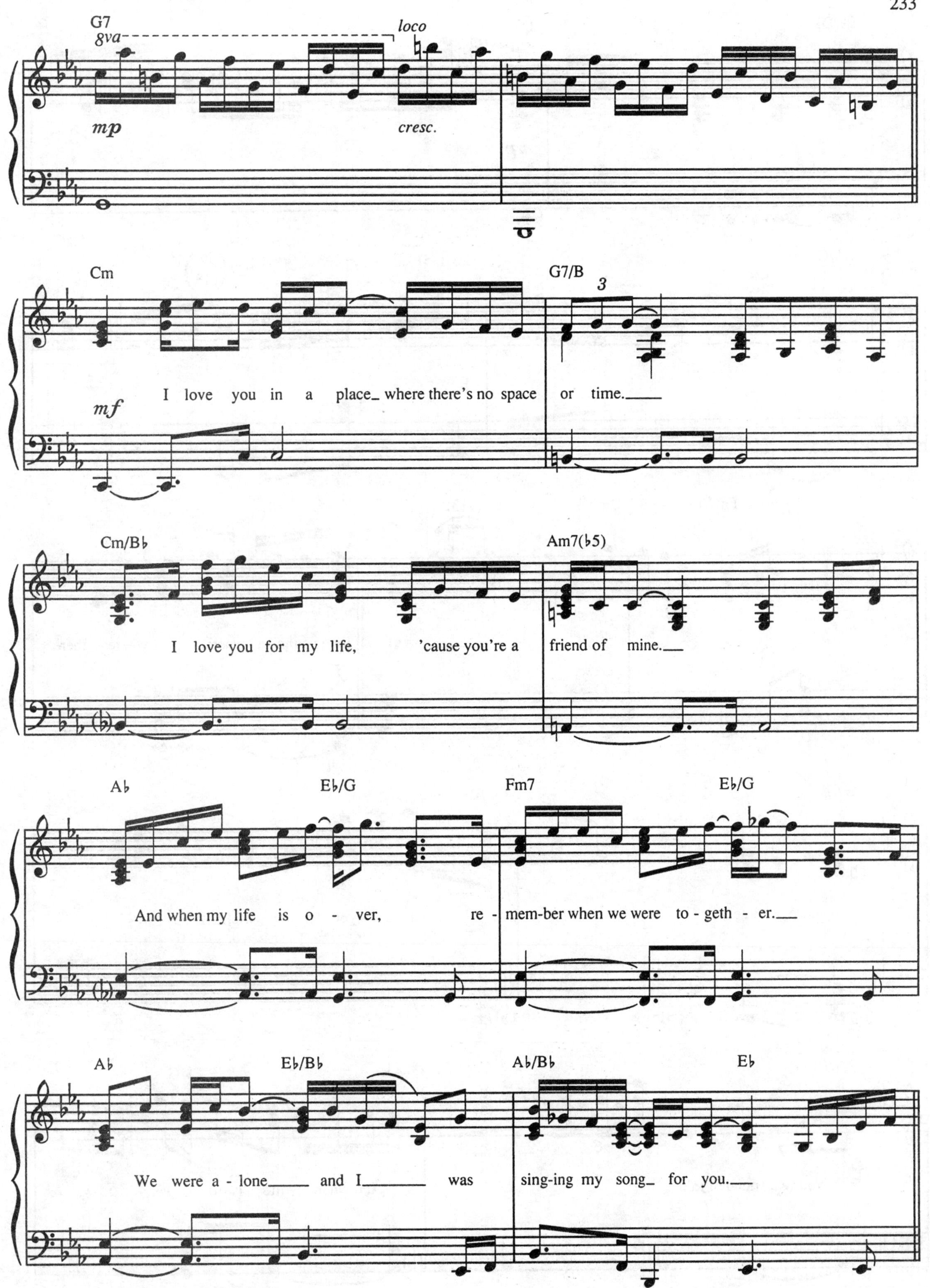
G7
8va
loco
mp
cresc.
Cm
G7/B
3
mf
I love you in a place_ where there's no space or time.___
Cm/B♭
Am7(♭5)
I love you for my life, 'cause you're a friend of mine.___
A♭
E♭/G
Fm7
E♭/G
And when my life is o - ver, re - mem-ber when we were to - geth - er.___
A♭
E♭/B♭
A♭/B♭
E♭
We were a - lone___ and I___ was sing-ing my song_ for you.___

E♭/D♭
D♭
dim.
mp
A♭/C
Gm7(♭5)
C7(♯9 ♭13)
cresc.
Fm9
Fm7/E♭
Dm7(♭5)
G7(♭13)
Cm
mf
I
love you in a place where there's
cresc.
f
G7/B
Cm/B♭
no space or time.
I love you for my life,
Am7(♭5)
A♭
E♭/G
you're a friend of mine.
And when my life is o - ver, re -

Fm7
Eb/G
Ab
Eb/Bb
mem-ber when we were to-geth-er.
We were a - lone and I was
Ab/Bb
Eb
Ab
Eb/Bb
sing-ing my song for you.
Yes,
we were a - lone and I was
dim.
Ab/Bb
Eb
Ab
Eb/G
sing-ing this song for you.
Yeah,
we were a - lone and I was
mf
Db(2)
Ab
sing-ing my song,
sing-ing my song,
sing - ing my
Ab/Eb
Eb
Bb
song,
sing-ing my song,
sing-ing my
song.
dim.
mp
rit. e dim.
p
8va

SPANISH FLEA

By
JULIUS WECHTER

Bb
Bb7
Eb
Eb7
Ab
Db
Db7
Gb
F7
D7
G7
C7
B
F
mf
f
1.
2.

STRONG ENOUGH

Words and Music by
SHERYL CROW, KEVIN GILBERT, BRIAN MACLEOD,
DAVID RICKETTS, BILL BOTTRELL and DAVID BAERWALD

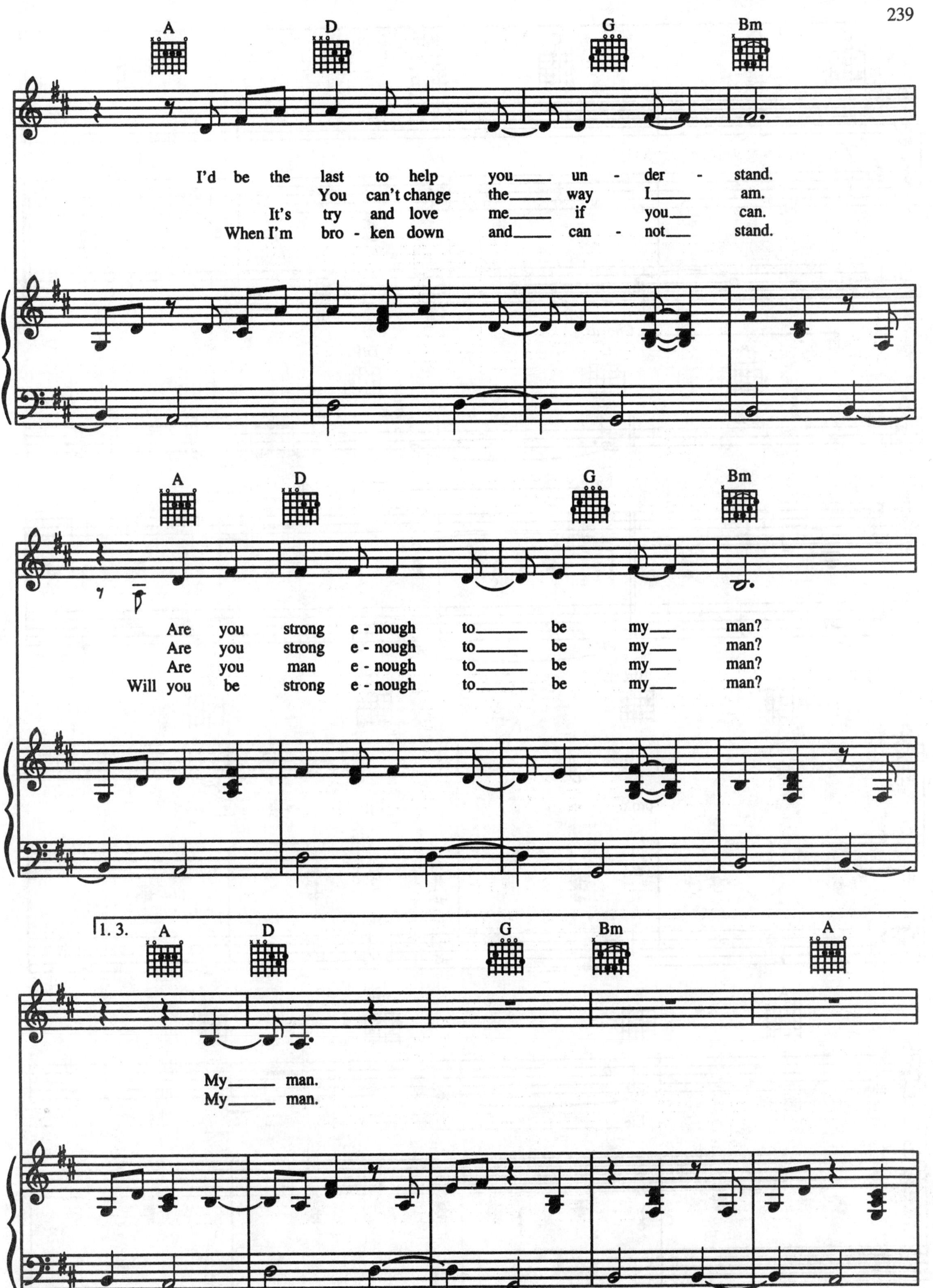
A
D
G
Bm
I'd be the last to help you un - der - stand.
You can't change the way I am.
It's try and love me if you can.
When I'm bro - ken down and can - not stand.
A
D
G
Bm
Are you strong e - nough to be my man?
Are you strong e - nough to be my man?
Are you man e - nough to be my man?
Will you be strong e - nough to be my man?
1. 3.
A
D
G
Bm
A
My man.
My man.

D G Bm A

2. 4.

Chorus:

A E D/F♯ G

Lie______ to me,______

A Bm C G

I promise I'll be - lieve.______

A E D/F♯ G

Lie______ to me,______

TAKE THE LONG WAY HOME

Words and Music by
ROGER HODGSON and
RICK DAVIES

Moderately
Cm7
B♭/C
p cresc.
mf
F/C
C
B♭/C
C
(Play 2x's)
Cm7
B♭/C
F/C
C
Verse
So you think you're a Ro - me - o playing a part in a pic - ture show, well take the
When lone-ly days turn to lone - ly nights you take a trip to the cit - y lights, and take the
mf
B♭/C
C
long way home, take the long way home.
long way home, take the long way home.

Cm7
B♭/C
F/C
C
Cause you're the joke of the neigh-bor-hood,
why should you care if you're feel-ing good, well take the
You nev-er see what you want to see,
for-ev-er play-ing to the gal-ler-y, you take the
B♭/C
C
long way home,
take the
long way home.
long way home,
take the
long way home.
Em7
Em7/D
Am
Em/G
Chorus
But there are times that you feel you're part
of the scen-er-y,
all the
And when you're up on the stage it's so
un-be-liev-a-ble,
un-for-
F
B♭
F/A
green-er-y
is com-in' down,
boy.
get-ta-ble
how they a-dore
you.

G
Em7
Am
Em/G
And then your wife seems to think you're part of the furn - i - ture,
oh it's pe -
But then your wife seems to think you're los - ing your san - i - ty,
oh it's ca -
F
B♭
F/A
to Coda
cu - li - ar,
she used to be
so
lam - i - ty,
oh is there no
way
1. G7
2. G7
E♭
3 fr.
B♭
nice.
out?
Oh!
ad lib Instrumental
F
C
B♭/C
1. C

2. C
D.S. 𝄋 (3rd Chorus)
al Coda
Coda
G7
time
Cm7
B♭/C
F/C
C
So, when the day comes to set - tle down
well, who's to blame if you're not a - round? You took the
B♭/C
A♭/C
long way home,
you took the long way home.
You took the
1. F/C
2. F/C
long way home,
you took the
long way home,
you took the

3rd Chorus

Well does it feel that your life's become
a catastrophe,
oh it has to be for you to grow, boy.
When you look through the years and see
what you could have been,
oh what you might have been if you had
had more time.

TEARS IN HEAVEN

Words and Music by
WILL JENNINGS and ERIC CLAPTON

C♯/E♯
A7/E
F♯
E/G♯
F♯7/A♯
and car - ry on, 'cause I know
through night and day, 'cause I know
Bm7
E7sus
A
E/G♯
F♯m
I don't be - long here in heav - en.
I just can't stay here in heav - en.
A/E
D/F♯
E7sus
E7
1.
A
2.
A
Bridge:
C
Bm7
Am7
D/F♯
Time can bring you down, time can bend your knees.

G
D/F♯
Em7
D/F♯
G
C
Bm7
Time can break your heart,
Am7
D/F♯
G
D/F♯
E
A/E
E7
have you beg - ging, "Please!"
Beg - ging, "Please!"
Verse:
A
E/G♯
F♯m
A/E
D/F♯
A/E
(Instrmental solo . . .
Would you know my name
if I saw you in heav -
E
A/E
E7
A
E/G♯
F♯m
A/E
en?
Would you be the same

D/F♯
A/E
E
A/E
E7
F♯m
if I saw you in heav - en?
. . . end solo)
Be-yond the door,
I must be strong
C♯/E♯
A7/E
F♯
E/G♯
F♯7/A♯
Bm7
there's peace I'm sure.
and car - ry on,
And I know there'll be no more
'cause I know I don't be-long
E7sus
A
E/G♯
F♯m
A/E
tears in heav - en.
here in heav - en.
1.
D/F♯
E7sus
E7
A
2.
D/F♯
E7sus
E7
A
molto rit.

THAT GIRL

Words and Music by
GARY BENSON, MAXI ELLIOT, ROBERT LIVINGSTON,
ORVILLE BURRELL, BOOKER T. JONES, STEVE CROPPER,
DONALD DUNN and AL JACKSON

F5
Ab
Bb
what she wants she won't let go. Takes you to the place of your fan - ta - sy, walks you to the door but she holds the key.
to click in ev - ery - thing you do. She can make you hot when it's cold outside, take you on a high, e - ven make you fly.
un - der pres - sure, she's smooth and sweet. No com - pli - ca - tions, just at - ti - tude. Be - lieves in what she's got and she won't get used.
That
Chorus:
girl, ooh, that kind of girl.
(Shaggy - ad lib:)
Gang - ster type of lov - er.
That girl, ooh, that

1.3.
2.4.5.
F5
A♭
B♭
kind of girl.
Smooth type of girl.
2. No mat-
3. She's
Mm...
Bridge:
1.4. She's out - spo - ken, I'm heart - bro - ken. Just the kind of girl to keep your
2.3. See additional lyrics
love life roll - ing. She's out - spo - ken, I'm heart - bro - ken.
To Coda
1.
2.
D.S.
Just the kind of girl to keep my... that, that, that... life com - plete.
That

3.

Verse:

F5 A♭ B♭ N.C.

man then, *oh, ah.* 4. Ho - ly Mo - ses, Lord, it could have been me.

Caught up in the rap and did - n't wan - na be. But I ain't no fool, I was one step a - head. I had to let go 'cause I was o - ver my head. That

D.S. 𝄋 al Coda

Coda

F5 A♭ B♭ F5 A♭ B♭ F5 A♭ B♭

that. That girl, ooh, that

Bridge 2:
That girl to make you break your silence and speak.
Just a glimpse upon the silhouette makes my knees get weak.
Baby, baby, so unique, a reggaematic,
Lover, lover, make her life complete.
(To Chorus:)

Bridge 3:
Well, I'm weak to her touch,
So vulnerable to her blush, love struck.
That girl, I got an instant crush.
You can call me a lush, infatuation or just lust.
The girl possess the stuff to make the man, then, oh, ah...
(To Chorus:)

Shaggy's ad-lib:
Gangster kind of lover,
'Cause she's the shaggy kind of girl.
I got to let them know.
Sexy kind of lover,
Maxi kind of girl.
I got to let them know,
She's the kind of girl that captivates your soul.
A rude girl type of love.
Shaggy and Maxi Priest definitely on the girl them case.

THINKING OF YOU

Words and Music by
JIM MESSINA

Moderately
D
Dmaj7
mf
Some-thin' in-side_ of me is tak-in' a hold_ each day,
some-thin' in - side___ of me is mak - in' me feel this way, when -

A
A sus4
A
A sus4
A
D
Dmaj7
ev-er you're near_ me, you've got me think-in' of you.___
D
Dmaj7
D
Dmaj7
D
Dmaj7
Some-thin' a-bout your eyes that won't let me look_ a-way,_
D
Dmaj7
D
Dmaj7
some-thin' a-bout your smile that's mak-in' it hard to say, when-
A
A sus4
A
A sus4
A
D
Dmaj7
ev-er you're near_ me, you've got me think-in' of you.___

D7
F#7
G
Gmaj7
Em7
F°
You know you've got me sing-in' a song, when-
D
G
Gmaj7
ev-er you're a-round me I just want to be-long to you, I would give
To Coda
Em7
F°
E7
D6
G°
3fr.
E7
A
Em7
Cm6
A7
all of my love, I wish that I could tell you, oh, what I'm think-in' of.
D
Dmaj7
D
Dmaj7
D
Dmaj7
D
Dmaj7

A
Asus4
A
Asus4
A
D
Dmaj7
D7
F#7
D. S. 𝄋
al Coda
You know
Coda
Cm6
A7
D
Dmaj7
Some - thin' in - side of me won't
D
Dmaj7
D
Dmaj7
let me be - gin the day,
some - thin' in - side of me is
D
Dmaj7
A
Asus4
mak - in' it hard to say
when - ev - er you're near me,

A
A sus4
A
D
D maj7
1.
D
D maj7
you've got me think-in' of you,
When -
2.
D
D maj7
A
A sus4
A
A sus4
A
When - ev - er you're near me,
you've got me think-in' of you,
D
D maj7
D
D maj7
A
A sus4
A
A sus4
A
you.
D
D maj7
D
D maj7
D
D maj7
D
D maj7
D

As Featured in the Motion Picture "MILK MONEY"
THIS HEART
Words and Music by
NANCI GRIFFITH
Rock ♩ = 120
(E) (A) (B) (E)
r.h. - play 2nd time only
mf
r.h. - play 2nd & 3rd time only
1.
2.3.
N.C.
Verse:
A B E
1. This heart was al - most taken.
2. This heart was born feet runnin'.
A B E A B
This heart had a love of it's own.
This heart saw your porch light on.
E A B E
This heart was re - a - wakened when you came a - long.
This heart hit the side - walk won-d'rin' why you left it on.

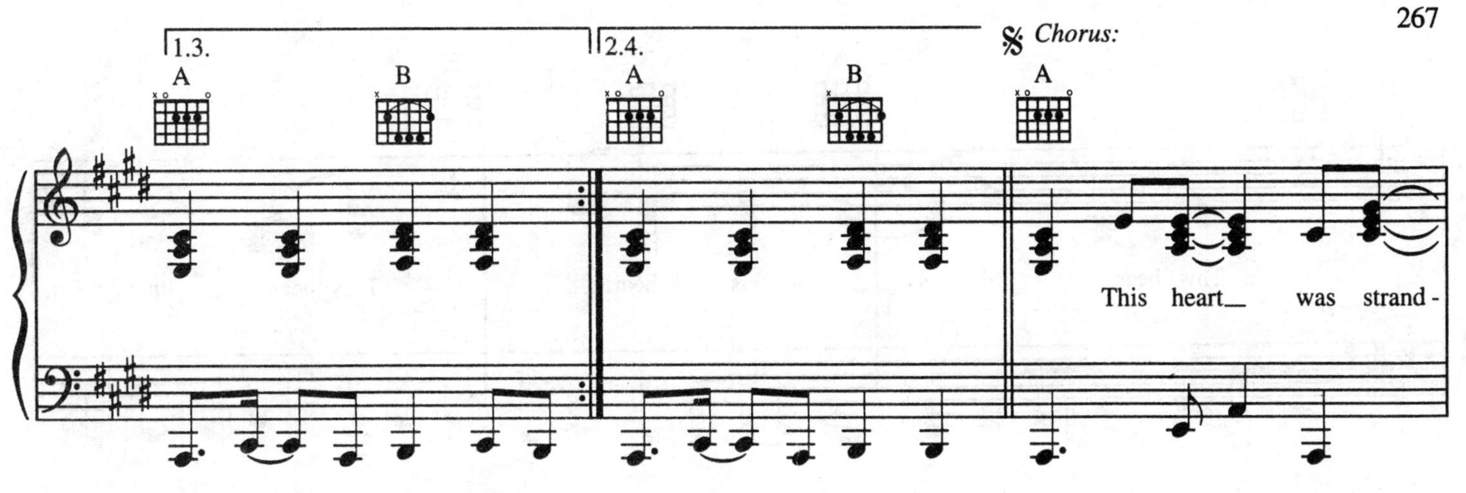
1.3.
2.4.
Chorus:
A
B
A
B
A
This heart was strand-

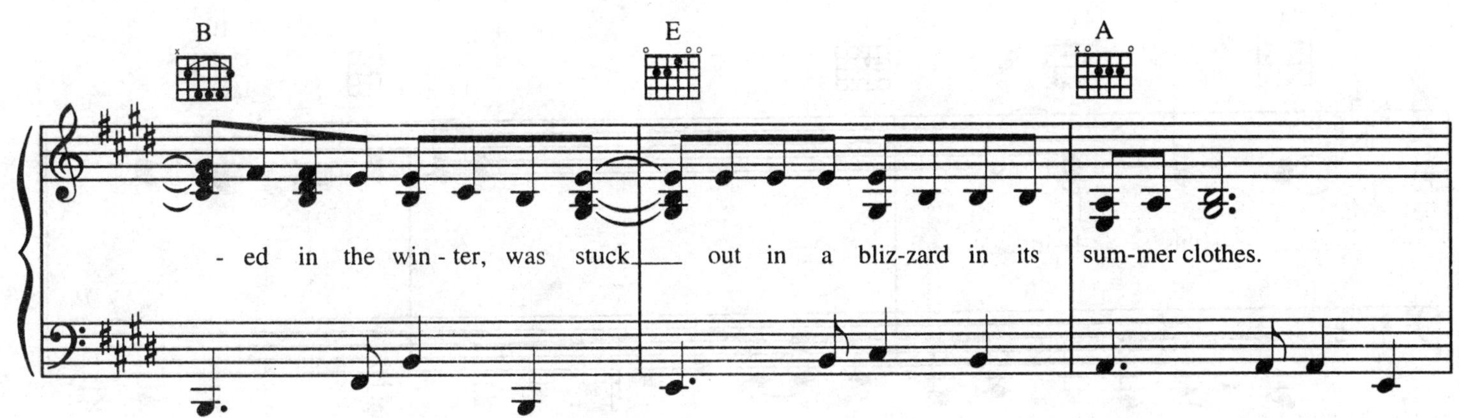
B
E
A
- ed in the win-ter, was stuck out in a bliz-zard in its sum-mer clothes.

B
E
To Coda
This heart knows when love comes and when it goes.

1.
D.C.
2.
E
A
B

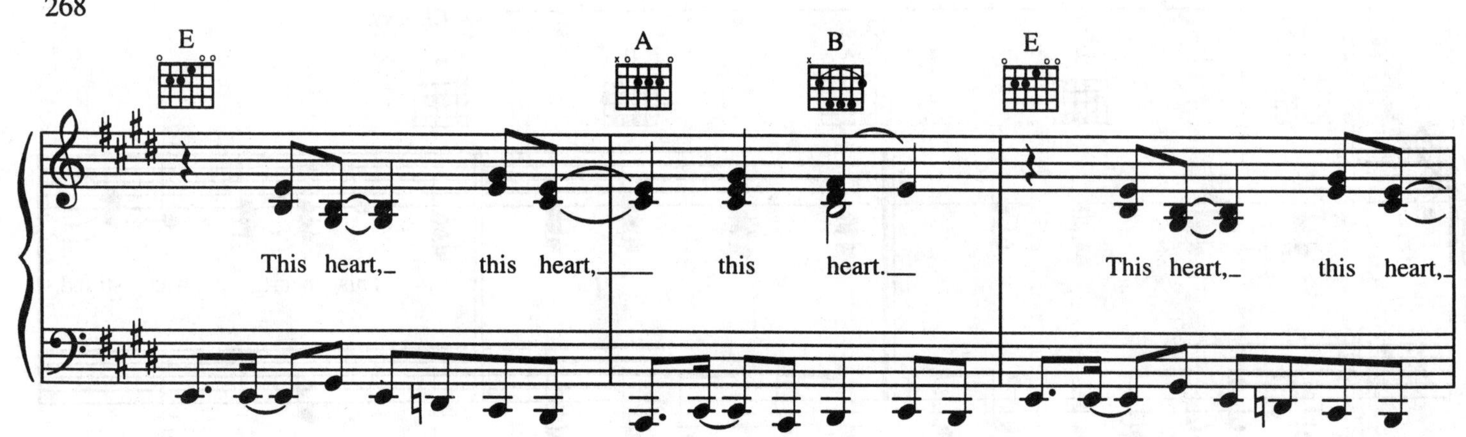
E
A
B
E
This heart,_ this heart,___ this heart.__
This heart,_ this heart,_

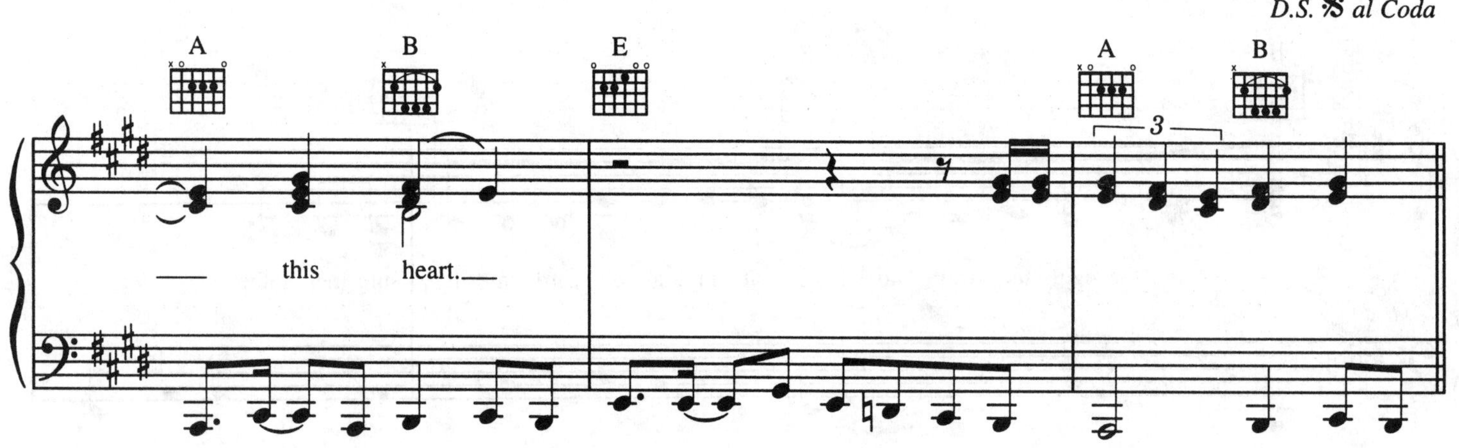
D.S. 𝄋 al Coda
A
B
E
A
B
3
___ this heart.__

Coda
Verse:
E
A
B
This heart_ was al - most_ tak-en.

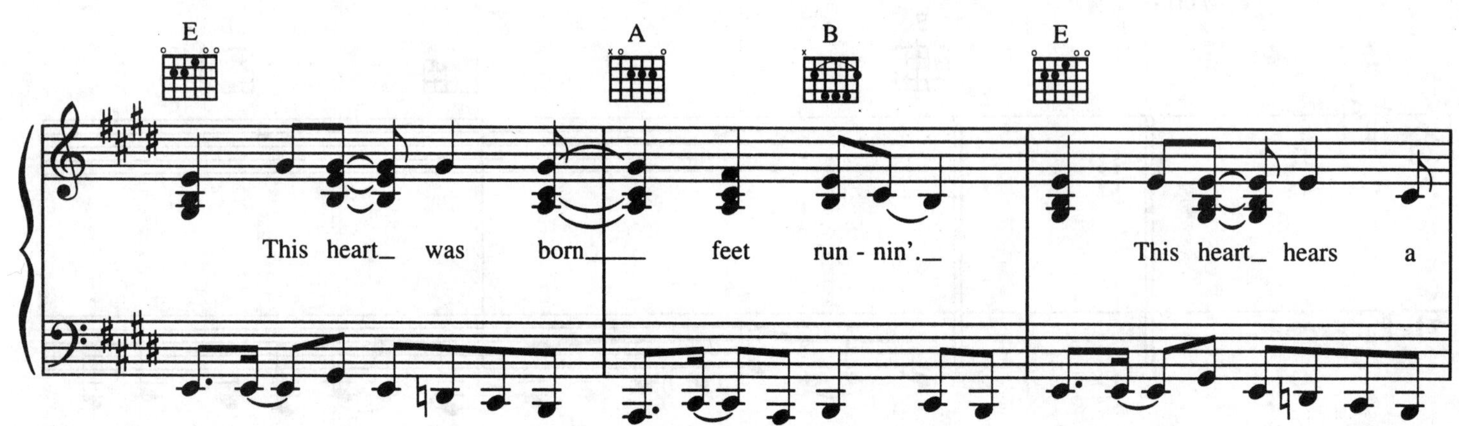
E
A
B
E
This heart_ was born___ feet run - nin'._
This heart_ hears a

A B E A B

tel - e - phone ring - in', gon - na let it go.

E A B E

This heart, this heart, this heart. This heart, this heart,

A B E A B E

this heart. This heart, this heart, this heart.

Verse 3:
This heart hears the telephone ringin'.
This heart is gonna let it go,
'Cuz this heart feels the bells she's hearin'
Aren't the telephone.

Verse 4:
This heart has heard your laughter.
This heart has learned how to smile.
This heart is your true believer
If you'll stay awhile.
(To Chorus:)

TOP OF THE WORLD

Lyric by
JOHN BETTIS

Music by
RICHARD CARPENTER

In Two
mp
D
A
G
D
Such a feel - in's com - in' ov - er me, there is
Some-thing in the wind has learned my name, and it's
mf

F#m Em A7 D

won - der in most ev - 'ry-thing I see, not a
tell - in' me that things are not the same, in the

G A F#m B7

cloud in the sky got the sun in my eyes, and I
leaves on the trees and the touch of the breeze, there's a

Em7 Em7-5 A(sus4) A

won't be sur-prised if it's a dream.
pleas - in' sense of hap - pi - ness for me.

D A G D

Ev - 'ry - thing I want the world to be, is now
There is on - ly one wish on my mind, when this

F#m
Em
A7
D
coming true e - spe - cial - ly for me, and the
day is through I hope that I will find, that to -
G
A
F#m
B7
rea - son is clear, it's be - cause you are here, you're the
mor - row will be just the same for you and me, all I
Em7
Em7-5
A (sus4)
A
near - est thing to heav - en that I've seen.
need will be mine if you are here. I'm on the
D
G
top of the world look - in' down on cre - a - tion and the

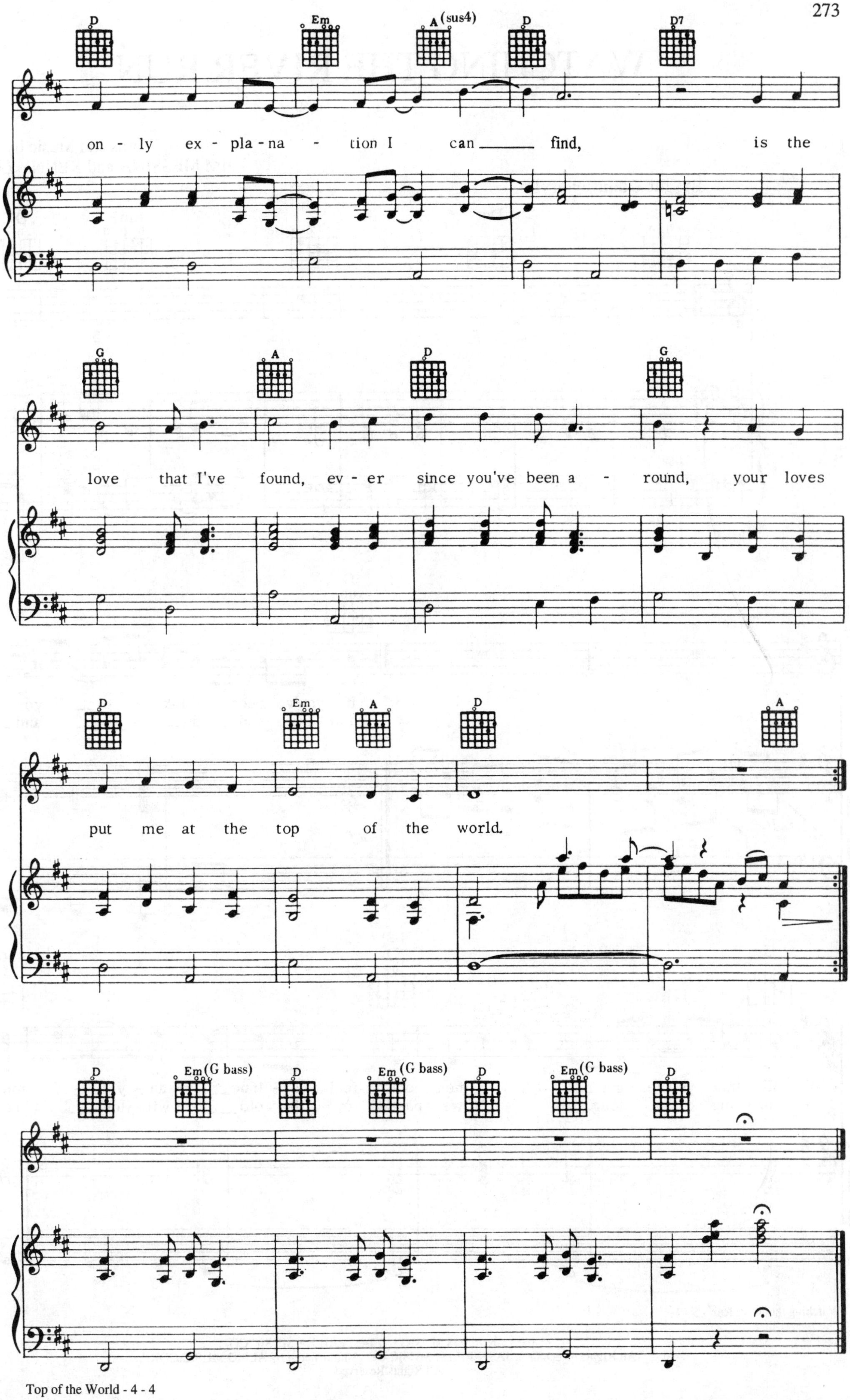

D Em A(sus4) D D7

on - ly ex - pla - na - tion I can find, is the

G A D G

love that I've found, ev - er since you've been a - round, your loves

D Em A D A

put me at the top of the world.

D Em(G bass) D Em(G bass) D Em(G bass) D

WATCHING THE RIVER RUN

Words and Music by
JIM MESSINA and KENNY LOGGINS

D7
G
C
'Cause when we're to-geth - er then you've got a lot 'cause
where lov-ers ca-ress as we sing them our song, re-
D7
G
I am the riv-er and you are the shore.
joic-ing to-geth-er when we greet the sea.
G7
C
D
And it goes on and on,
G
D
Csus2
G
C
watch-ing the riv-er run fur-ther and fur-

C/B
Am7
D
G
ther from things that we've_ done, leav - ing them_ one_ by_
G7
C
D
one. And we have- just be - gun
G
Dm
E7
Am7
watch-ing the riv - er_ run,_ lis-ten-ing and learn-
C
D
G
1.
Dm
ing and_ yearn- ing to run, riv - er,_ run._
mp

2.
C
Am7
D7
Tacet
G7
And it goes
cresc.
D
G
on and on, watching the river
f
Csus2
C/B
run further and further from things that we've
done, leaving them one by one. And we have

C
D
B7
just be - gun watch-ing the riv - er
Em
Gmaj7
C
Am7
D
run, lis-ten-ing and learn-ing and yearn-ing to
G
Dm
C
run, riv - er, run.
mf gradual dim.
Am7
D
Tacet
G

WE'VE ONLY JUST BEGUN

Words by
PAUL WILLIAMS

Music by
ROGER NICHOLS

Cm9
Cm7
Fm9
To Coda
A kiss for luck_ and we're on our way._
We start out walk - ing and learn to run._
We'll find a place_ where there's room to grow._
1.
Bb7 (sus) - Bb7
2.3.
Bb7 (sus)
Ebmaj7
Abmaj7
And yes, We've Just Be - gun._
Ebmaj7
Abmaj7
Bb
C
Fmaj7
C
Fmaj7
Shar-ing hor-i-zons that are new to us,
C
Fmaj7
Cmaj7
Fmaj7
E
Amaj7
watch-ing the signs a-long the way.
Talk-ing it ov-er just the

E
Amaj7
E
Amaj7
two of us, working together day to
Bb7(sus)
Bb9(sus)
2.
3
Bb9(sus)
day, together.
gether,
to-
D.S. al Coda
gether.
Coda
Bb7(sus)
Ebmaj7
And yes, We've Just Begun.
Abmaj7
Ebmaj9
Abmaj7
G

WE DON'T NEED ANOTHER HERO
(Thunderdome)

Words and Music by
GRAHAM LYLE and TERRY BRITTEN

F♯
C♯no3rd
1.3.
mis - take this time.
they left be - hind.
Bridge I:
2.4.
E
F♯
C♯m9
cresc. And I
won - der when we are
ev - er gon - na
change;
mf
living
un - der the fear till
noth - ing else re - mains.
Chorus:
Emaj7/G♯
f We don't need an - oth - er
he - ro.
We don't need to know the
way home.
F♯/D♯
All we want is life be - yond to Thun - der -

Verse 3:
Looking for something we can rely on;
There's got to be something better out there.

Verse 4:
Love and compassion; that day is coming.
All else are castles built in the air.

(To Bridge I)

WHILE YOU SEE A CHANCE

Lyrics by
WILL JENNINGS

Music by
STEVE WINWOOD

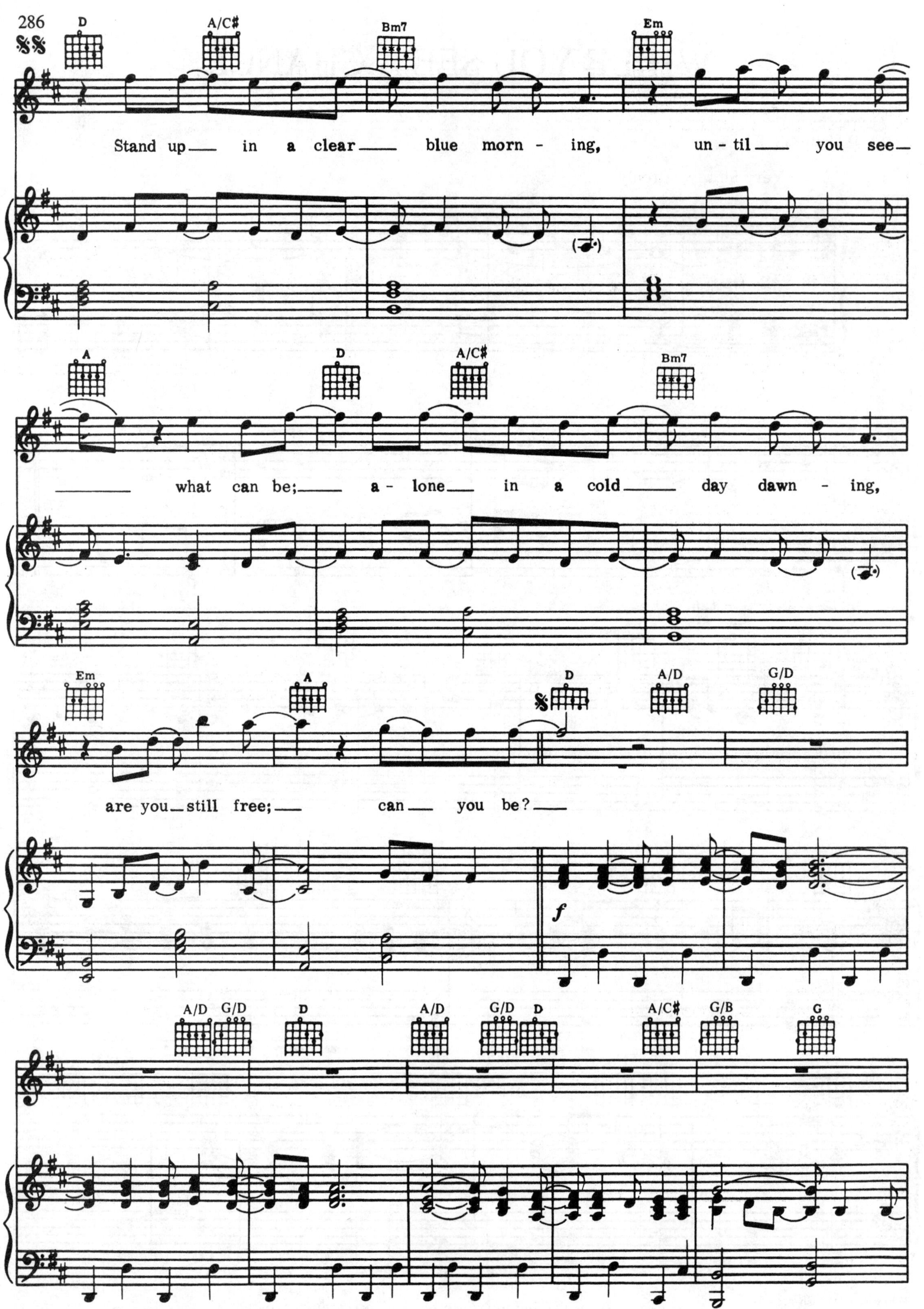
D
A/C♯
Bm7
Em
Stand up in a clear blue morn - ing, un - til you see
A
D
A/C♯
Bm7
what can be; a - lone in a cold day dawn - ing,
Em
A
D
A/D
G/D
are you still free; can you be?
f
A/D
G/D
D
A/D
G/D
D
A/C♯
G/B
G

Em7/A D G/B G D/A A F#m D9

G Gmaj7 Em9 D/A Gmaj7

When some cold to - mor - row finds ___ you; when some sad old dream re - minds ___
When there's no one left ___ to leave ___ you; e - ven you don't quite be - lieve ___
And that old, grey wind ___ is blow - ing; and there's noth - ing left worth know -

mp

D/A G E/G#

___ you how the end - less road ___ un - winds ___ you;
___ you; that's when noth - ing can ___ de - ceive ___ you;
ing; and it's time you should ___ be go - ing;

while you see ___

cresc.

D/A
F#/A#
Bm
a chance, take it; find ro - mance, fake
D/C
Bm
G/B
A7
To Coda
it; be - cause it's all on you.
D
1. to next strain
2. D.S.S. al Coda
Bb
F/Bb
Eb/Bb
Don't you know
F/Bb
Bb
F/Bb
Eb/Bb
by now, no one gives you an - y - thing;

B♭
F/B♭
E♭/B♭
F/E♭
C/G
D/A
and don't you won - der how you keep — on mov - ing
cresc.
A7sus
D.S.
one more day, your way?
D
Em/D
1.
2.
While you
Repeat ad lib and fade
see a chance, take it; find ro - mance; while you

WHAT'S LOVE GOT TO DO WITH IT

Words and Music by
TERRY BRITTEN and
GRAHAM LYLE

Verse:
Em7
G♯m7
must un - der - stand that the touch of your hand makes my
mp
D/E
F♯/G♯
Em7
G♯m7
pulse re - act; that it's on - ly the thrill of
D/E
F♯/G♯
boy meet - ing girl; op - po - sites at - tract. It's
C
E
D
F♯
C
E
D
F♯
phys - i - cal, on - ly log - i - cal,
mf

C
E
D
F♯
you must try to ig - nore that it means more than that. Oh,
cresc.
Chorus:
Em
G♯m
N.C.
what's love got to do, got to do with it? What's love but a
f
sec - ond hand e - mo - tion? What's love got to do,
got to do with it? Who needs a heart when a

1.
2.
C
D
E
F♯
heart can be bro - ken? It
heart can be bro - ken.
F♯m
Bbm
Ab
Gb
N.C.
instrumental solo ad lib.
G/A
Cb/Db
I've been tak - ing on a
mf

A
G/A
A
Db
Cb/Db
Db
new di - rec - tion, but I have to say,
F
G/F
A
B/A
I've been think - ing 'bout my own pro - tec - tion; it
Em7
A
F#m
E
Abm7
Db
N.C.
Bbm
Ab
scares me to feel this way. Oh, what's love got to do
bro - ken.
D
E
F#m
E
Gb
Ab
N.C.
Bbm
Ab
got to do with it? What's love but a

Verse 2:
It may seem to you
That I'm acting confused
When you're close to me.
If I tend to look dazed,
I read it some place;
I've got cause to be.
There's a name for it,
There's a phrase that fits,
But whatever the reason,
You do it for me.

(To Chorus)

WHEN THE NIGHT COMES

Lyrics and Music by
BRYAN ADAMS, JIM VALLANCE
& DIANE WARREN

Rock ♩= 84
A♭
G♭
D♭
G♭
mp
with Pedal

A♭
G♭
D♭
G♭

A♭
G♭
D♭
D♭/E♭
A♭
G♭
D♭
D♭/E♭

Verse:
A♭
G♭
D♭
G♭
1. Hold on.
I'll be back for you, it won't be long.

A♭
G♭
D♭
G♭
But for now, there's some-thing out there call-ing me.
A♭
G♭
D♭
G♭
So, take me down that lone-some road. Point me east and let me go.
A♭
G♭
D♭
D♭/E♭
This suit-case weighs me down with mem-o-ries. I just
cresc.
mf
Chorus:
A♭
G♭
D♭
D♭/E♭
wan-na be the one you run to, I just wan-na be the one you come to. I just
A♭
G♭
D♭
D♭/E♭
wan-na be there with some-one when the night comes. Let's

A♭
G♭
D♭
D♭/E♭
put all our cares be-hind us, and go where they'll nev-er find us. I just
A♭
G♭
1.
D♭
wan-na be there be-side you when the night comes, when the night comes.
D.S. 𝄋
A♭
G♭
D♭
G♭
A♭
G♭
D♭
G♭
dim.
mp
2.
To Next Strain
3.
Repeat ad lib. and fade
D♭
D♭
night comes, when the night comes.
cresc.
night comes, when the night comes. I just

Bridge:
B♭m
D♭
B♭m
I know there'll be a time for
you and I,
just take my hand and run a -
f
D♭
E♭m
way.
Pick up all the piec - es of this
B♭m
G♭
shat-tered dream,
we're gon-na
make it ours some - day.
That's when we're
D.S. 𝄋
A♭
com-in' back,
com-in' back to stay.

Verse 2:
Two spirits in the night,
We could leave before the morning light.
When there's nothin' left to lose,
There's nothin' left to fear.
So meet me on the edge of town.
Won't keep you waitin', I'll be 'round.
Then, you and I, we'll just roll right outa here.
To Chorus:

Verse 3: (Instrumental Solo)
To Chorus:

Recorded by THE JERRERSON AIRPLANE

WHITE RABBIT

Words and Music by
GRACE SLICK

G
C
just had some kind of mush - room, and your mind is mov - ing low, Go ask
Am
A-lice I think she'll know. When lo - gic and pro -
Am
B♭
Am
por - tion have fal - len slop - py dead, And the White Knight is talk - ing
B♭
C
E♭
back-wards, and the Red Queen's lost her head, Re - mem - ber what the Dor - mouse
f
ff
C
G
C
G
C
said. Feed your head, feed your head.

From the Motion Picture Soundtrack "Murder Was the Case"

WOMAN TO WOMAN

Words and Music by
JAMES BANKS, EDDIE MARION
and HENDERSON THIGPEN

Intro. monologue:
E♭maj9
Cm7
Spoken: (See additional lyrics)
E♭maj9
Cm7
E♭maj9
Cm7
E♭maj9
Cm7

E♭maj9
Cm7
E♭maj9
Cm7
E♭maj9
Cm7
Fm7/B♭

Verse 1:

Ebmaj9 Abmaj9 Ebmaj9

1.Wom-an to wom - an, have you ev - er been in love?__ Then you will know__

Cm7 Eb7 Abmaj9 Ebmaj9 Abmaj9

how I__ feel.__ Wom-an to wom - an, now if you were in my shoes,

Ebmaj9 Fm7/Bb

wouldn't you have done______ the same thing_ too?__ Wom -

Chorus:

Ebmaj9 Abmaj9

- an______ to wom - an,_____ can't you see where I'm com-ing from?

Ebmaj9
Abmaj9
Wom-an to wom - an ain't that the same thing you would have done.
Ebmaj9
Abmaj9
Wom - an to wom - an, why should I just step a - side
Ebmaj9
Fm7/Bb
and let you have what's right-ful-ly mine?
Verses 2 & 3:
Ebmaj9
Abmaj9
2.Wom - an to wom - an, I don't know I'm right, I can be wrong.
3. See additional lyrics.

E♭maj9 Cm7 E♭7 A♭maj9

I ain't gon-na let noth - in' break up my hap - py home.

E♭maj9 A♭maj9

Wom-an to wom - an to wom - an, use your self - con - trol now,

1.

E♭maj9 Fm7/B♭

you have to un - der - stand, I love that man, and he's

2.

Fm7/B♭ E♭maj9

mine. give him up. You bet-ter be-lieve I ain't ly-ing. Wom - an to wom-an

A♭maj9
E♭maj9
Cm7
E♭m7
A♭maj9
I just want you to un-der-stand. I'd do an - y - thing to keep my man.
E♭maj9
Cm7
1.Wom - an, wom - an,
2. Vocal ad lib.
E♭maj9
Cm7
you know that man is mine.
E♭maj9
Cm7
I ain't gon-na give him up. Yeah.

E♭maj9
1.
Cm7
I ain't gon-na give him up, and I ain't gon-na let you break up...
2.
Cm7
E♭maj9
love my man.
rit.

Intro. Monologue:

Hello? Hello? May I speak to Yolanda. Yeah, Yolanda, what's up? This is Juade. I know you know who I am 'cause I just ★ 69'ed you back. The reason you dialed my number, I don't know, but there ain't no man livin' here. This is my place, hoe. So, woman to woman, I didn't think it was being any more than fair for me to call you back and let you know how I was feeling. See, Yolanda, the truth is I don't give a damn about how you're taking this, 'cause a real woman wouldn't be sitting out there trying to play on nobody's phone anyway. But it really doesn't make any difference. I felt it was only right for me to let you know that the man you're in love with is sprung on the rebound, from the top of his head to the bottom of his feet. I'm what he loves and he loves the food that he eats. You see these rings on my fingers? They're yours. I got a brand new car and you own a bus. Yolanda, check this out...

Verse 3:
I'm talkin' to you woman to woman,
Now you should understand,
I'd do anything to keep my man
And I ain't gonna give 'im up.
I'm talkin' to you woman to woman,
Woman to woman,
He's mine and I ain't gonna give him up.
You better believe I ain't lyin'.

WOULDN'T IT BE NICE?

Words by
BRIAN WILSON and TONY ASHER
Music by
BRIAN WILSON
G9
C
F6
Am7
Would-n't it be nice if we were old - er_ Then_ we would-n't have to wait_ so_
nice if we could wake_ up_ In_ the morn-ing when the day_ is_
Dm
G9
C
long___ And would-n't it be nice to live to - ge - ther In_ the kind of
new___ And af - ter that to spend the day to - ge - ther Hold_ each oth - er
F6
Am7
Dm
G9
Am7
C11
world where we'd_ be - long___
close the whole_ night_ through_
Though it's gon-na make it that much bet - ter
The hap - py times to-geth-er we'd been spend-ing_
Am
Em
Dm7
1 G9
When we can say good-night and stay to - geth - er___
I wish that ev-'ry kiss was nev - er end - ing_
Would-n't it be

2 G9 G11 C A

Oh would-n't it __ be nice. ____ Well may-be if ___ we
Ba-by then __ there

D C#m 1 F#m7 2 F#m7

think and wish and hope and pray it might come true ___
would-n't be a sin-gle thing we could-n't __ do ___ We could be mar-

C#m7 F#m7 C#m7 G9 G11

-ried ___ and then we'd be hap-py ___ Oh would-n't it __ be __

C

Repeat and fade

__ nice. ___

YOU AND ME AGAINST THE WORLD

Words and Music by
PAUL WILLIAMS and
KEN ASCHER

Fm
C7
cir - cus came to town
and you were fright-ened by the clown
C7-9
C7+
Fm7
Bb7
was-n't it nice to be a-round
some - one that you knew
Ebm7
Ab13
Dbmaj7
some-one who was big and strong and
look-in' out for you
and me a-gainst the world.
Gbmaj7
Dbmaj9
C7
F7
some-times it feels like you and me a-gainst the world
and for all
Bbm7
Db7
Gdim
the times we've cried
I al-ways felt the odds were on our side.

C7
Fm
Db7
And when one of us is gone and one is left a -
Gb6
Gbm6
Fm7
lone to car-ry on well then re - mem-ber-ing will have to do
Ebm7
Fm7-5
Bb7
our mem-o-ries a - lone will get us through. Think a-bout the
Ebm7
Ab7
Dbmaj7
days of me and you of you and me a-gainst the world.
Dbmaj7
C7
Fm
Life can be a cir - cus they un - der

C7
Fm7
pay and ov - er work us
and though we sel - dom get our due
Bb7
Ebm7
Ab13
when each day is through
I bring my tir-ed bo - dy home and look a-round _ for me ___ and
Dbmaj7
Gbmaj7
Dbmaj7
you ___ a-gainst the world
some-times it feels like you and me a-gainst the world.
C7
Bbm7
Db7
And for all ___ the times we've cried
I al-ways felt that God was on our

Gdim
C7
Fm
side.
And when one of us is gone
Db7
Gb6
Gbm6
and one is left a - lone to car-ry on
well then re -
Fm7
Ebm7
Fm7-5
mem-ber-ing will have to do
our mem-o-ries a - lone will get us through.
Bb7
Ebm7
Ab7
Think a-bout the days of me and you
of you and me a-gainst the
Dbmaj7
Gbmaj7
Dbmaj7
Gbmaj7
Bbmaj7
world.

YOU ARE SO BEAUTIFUL

Words and Music by
BILLY PRESTON and
BRUCE FISHER

F
Cm7
F7 (+9)
B♭
me. Can't you see (2nd-sing) you're ev-'ry-thing that I
mf
A
Dm
G9
B♭m6
hope for and what's more, you're ev-'ry-thing I need.
f
F (C bass)
(C bass) Fmaj7
(C bass) F7
B♭
B♭m
F
B♭ (F bass)
F
(C bass) B♭
C7
You Are So Beau-ti-ful ba-by to me.
mp
F
Fmaj7
F7
B♭
B♭m
F
B♭
Such joy and hap-pi-ness you bring. (I wan-na thank you babe.)

F
(C bass)
B♭
C7
F
Fmaj7
F7
B♭
B♭m
Such joy and hap-pi-ness you
bring, just like a dream.
Cm7
F7
B♭
You're like a guid-ing light
mf
A
Dm
shin-in' in the night, you're hea-ven still to
f
G9
B♭m6
F (C bass)
Fmaj7
F7 (C bass)
B♭
B♭m
me. (Hey babe,) You Are So Beau-ti-ful.
mp

YOU MAKE ME FEEL LIKE DANCING

Words and Music by
LEO SAYER and VINCENT PONCIA

Gm7
3 fr.
C11
F
Dm7
Gm7
3 fr.
C11
walk - ing like a dog hang-ing on your lead.
the light, 'cause I don't wan - na go home.
Eb
F
I'm in a spin, you know; shak - ing on a string, you know.
You put a spell on me; I'm right where you want me to be.
cresc.
G
3 fr.
G/F#
G/E
G/D
Am7
D11
You make me feel like dan - ing; I wan-na dance the night a-way.
f
G
3 fr.
G/F#
G/E
G/D
Am7
D11
You make me feel like dan - ing; I'm gon-na dance the night a-way.

G
G/F♯
G/E
G/D
Am7
D11
3 fr.
You make me feel like_ danc - ing. I feel_ like
Gm7
3 fr.
1.
C11
danc - ing,_ danc - ing,_ dance the night_ a-way. I feel like danc - ing,_ danc - ing,_ ah._
2. C11
danc - ing,_ danc - ing,_ dance the night_ a - way. I feel like
Gm7
3 fr.
C11
danc - ing,_ danc - ing,_ dance the night_ a - way. I feel like danc - ing,_ danc - ing,_ ah._

1. 2.
F
Dm7
Gm7
3 fr.
C11
mf
3.
Gm7
3 fr.
C11
E♭
F
And if you'll let me stay, we'll dance our lives a - way.
cresc.
Repeat and fade
G
G/F♯
G/E
G/D
Am7
D11
3 fr.
You make me feel like dancing; I wan-na dance my life a-way.
Repeat and fade
f
G
G/F♯
G/E
G/D
Am7
D11
3 fr.
You make me feel like dancing; I wan-na dance my life a-way.

YOUR LITTLE SECRET

Words and Music by
MELISSA ETHERIDGE
Moderately slow ♩ = 92
Verse:
A5 G5 D
C5 A
mf
1. I know what_ you're think - ing, ba - by.
2. Tell it to___ me soft - ly, ba - by,
A5 G5 D/F♯
I used to___ be just_ like you.___
you nev - er meant no one_ no harm.__
You move when she's_ not look-ing, ba - by,
Your won - der - land's_ a mir - ror, ba - by,
C5 A
Bm
one su - gar ain't_ e - nough_ for you. You,
it's swift-ly fad - ing like_ your charm. You,
you're tak - ing out_ your loans,
you're step-ping out_ of line,

D
A
you're bur - y - ing your bones.
Be-fore your cov - er's blown,
you're spill - ing all the wine.
Leave it on the vine,
C
E
A/E
E
A/E
you bet-ter take it home.
I can't give you mine.
I
Chorus:
A
D
G
D
like the way you look,
I know you like me.
But
A
D
G
D
A
D
one and one and one,
ba - by, makes three. Stop
play-ing those eyes
if

To Coda
1.
G
D
A
you want me to keep your lit - tle se - cret. Lit - tle se - cret, lit - tle se - cret, yeah.
2.
A
cret. Lit - tle se - cret, lit - tle se - cret, yeah. Lit - tle se - cret, lit - tle se - cret.
Bridge:
E
F
E
I could, I won't, I can't, I don't. You make it hard,
F
E
F
talk down my guard. My sen - ses soaked, my e - go's choked.

E
F
I will not lie, I will not lie,
G
G7(♯9)
I, I. I, I.
(♮)
A
D
G
D
Inst. solo ad lib....
A
D
G
D

A
D
G
D
A
D
G
D
D.S. 𝄋 al Coda
I
Coda
A
D
G
D
cret. Lit - tle se - cret, lit - tle se - cret, yeah. Lit - tle se - cret, lit - tle se - cret, yeah.
A
D
G
D
Lit - tle se - cret, lit - tle se - cret, yeah. Lit - tle se - cret, lit - tle se - cret, yeah.
2. Vocal ad lib.

A
D
G
D
Lit - tle se - cret, lit - tle se - cret, yeah. Lit - tle se - cret, lit - tle se - cret, yeah.
A
D
G
D
A
D
G
D
A5
G5
D
C5
A

YOUR MAMA DON'T DANCE

Words and Music by
JIM MESSINA and KENNY LOGGINS

Rock shuffle ♩=154

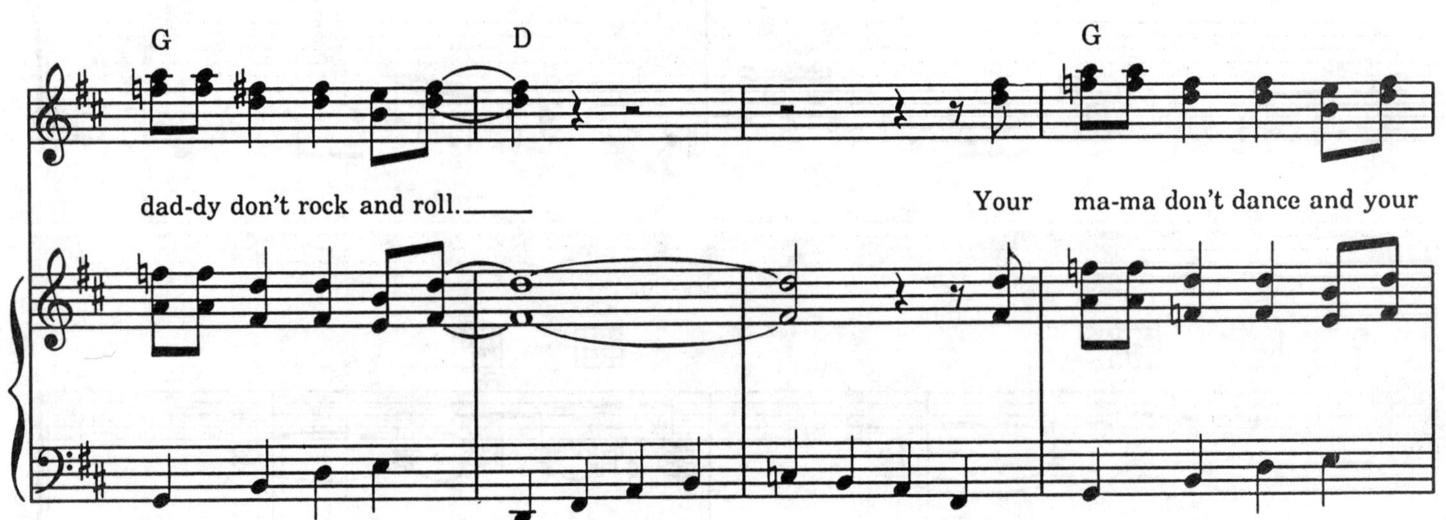

D
A
dad-dy don't rock and roll.
When eve - nin' rolls a-round and it's
G
D
time to hit the town, where do you go?
You've got to rock it!
The
3
D
G
D
old folks say that you got-ta end your day by ten,
mm-mm.
But if you're
G
D
out on a date don't you bring her home late, 'cause it's a sin.
You know

A
G
D
there's no ex-cuse, you know you're gon-na lose; you nev-er win; I'll say it a -
Chorus:
D
G
gain. And it's all be-cause your ma-ma don't dance and your da-dy don't rock and roll.
D
G
Your ma-ma don't dance and your
D
dad-dy don't rock and roll. When eve -

A
G
D
- nin' rolls a-round and it's time to hit the town, where do you go?
You've got to
3
3
rock it! Rock it!
D
G
D
Instr. solo ad lib...
G
D
To Coda
A
G
D

Bridge:
F♯
G
F♯
G
F♯
Yeah, we pull in - to a drive-in and I find a place to park. We
...solo ends
G
F♯
G
F♯
G
F♯
hop in - to the back seat, where I know it's nice and dark. We're just a - bout to move, think-in'
G
F♯
G
F♯
mmm yeah, this is a breeze. Then there's a light in my eye, and a guy says,
G N.C.
A
"Out - ta the car, long hair, but ooo - wee, you're com - in' with

D.S. 𝄋 al Coda
me to the lo - cal po-lice."
And it's all be-cause your

Coda
D
G
Your ma-ma don't dance and your dad - dy don't rock and roll.

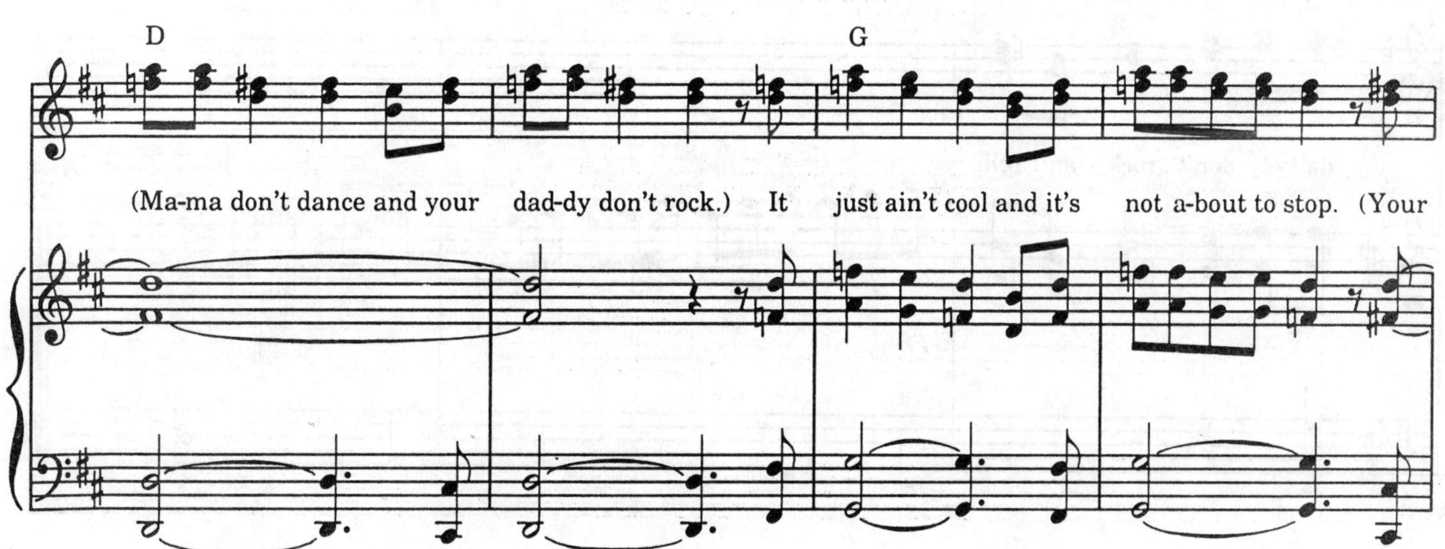
D
G
(Ma-ma don't dance and your dad-dy don't rock.) It just ain't cool and it's not a-bout to stop. (Your

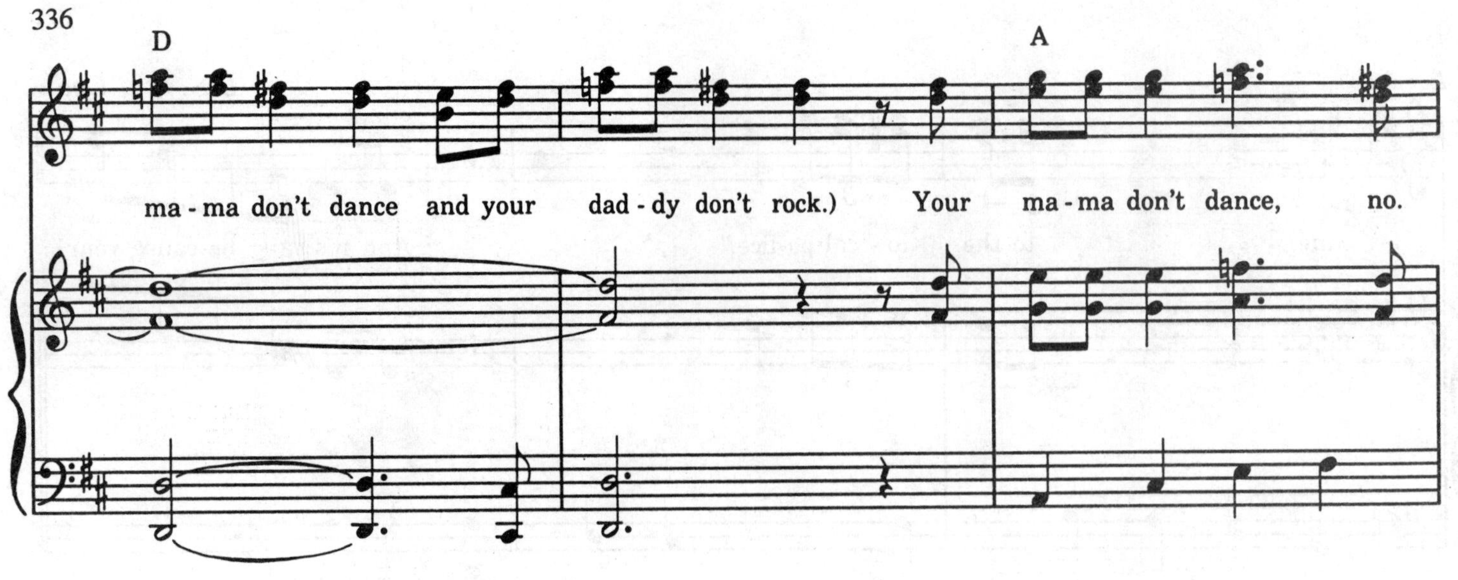
D
A
ma - ma don't dance and your dad - dy don't rock.) Your ma - ma don't dance, no.

G
A
G
A
She just don't dance, no. Your ma-ma don't dance and your

G
dad - dy don't rock and roll.
ff